Vunzi

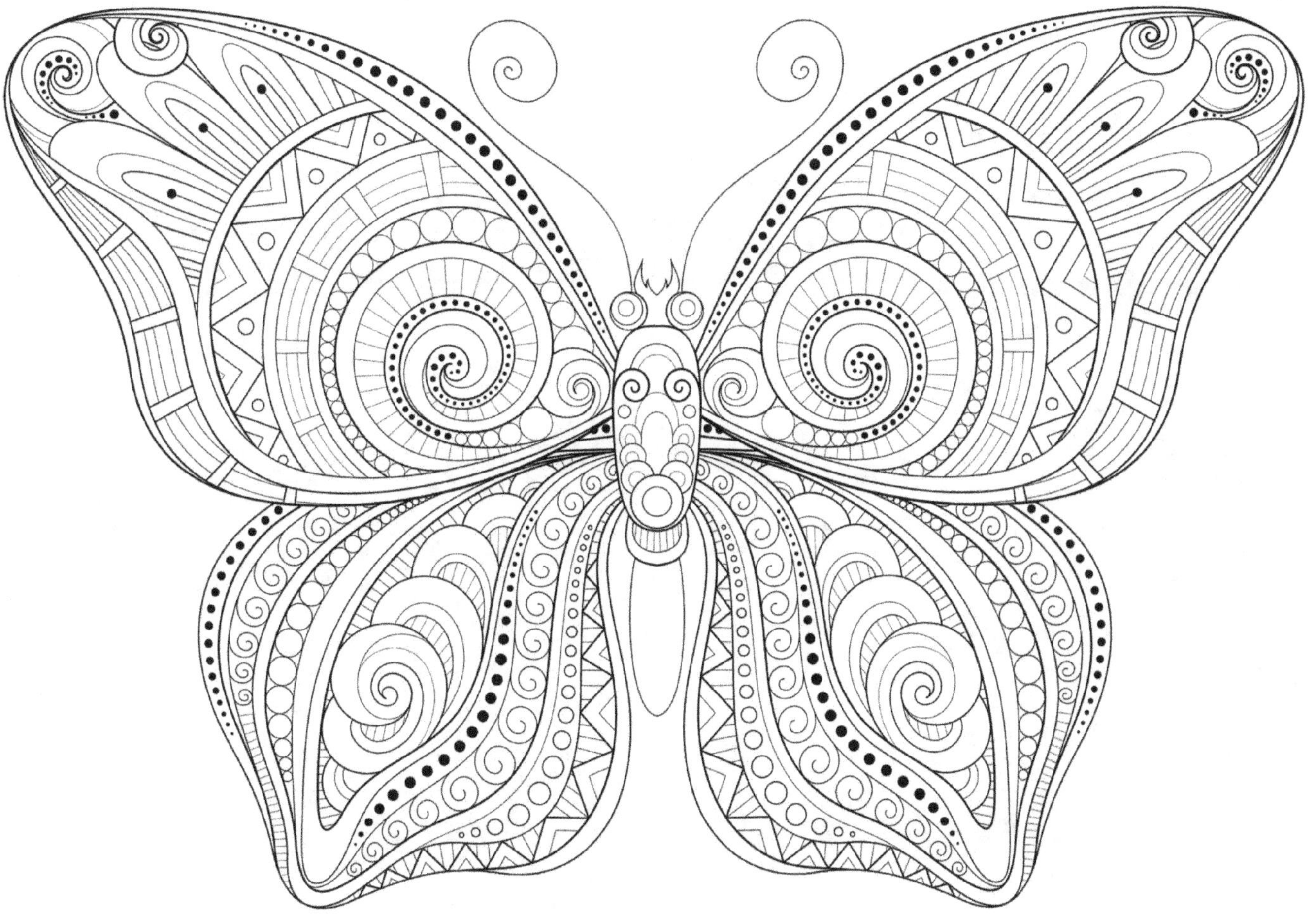

BUTTERFLY

Coloring Book For Adults

ISBN-13: 978-1-0821-3791-4

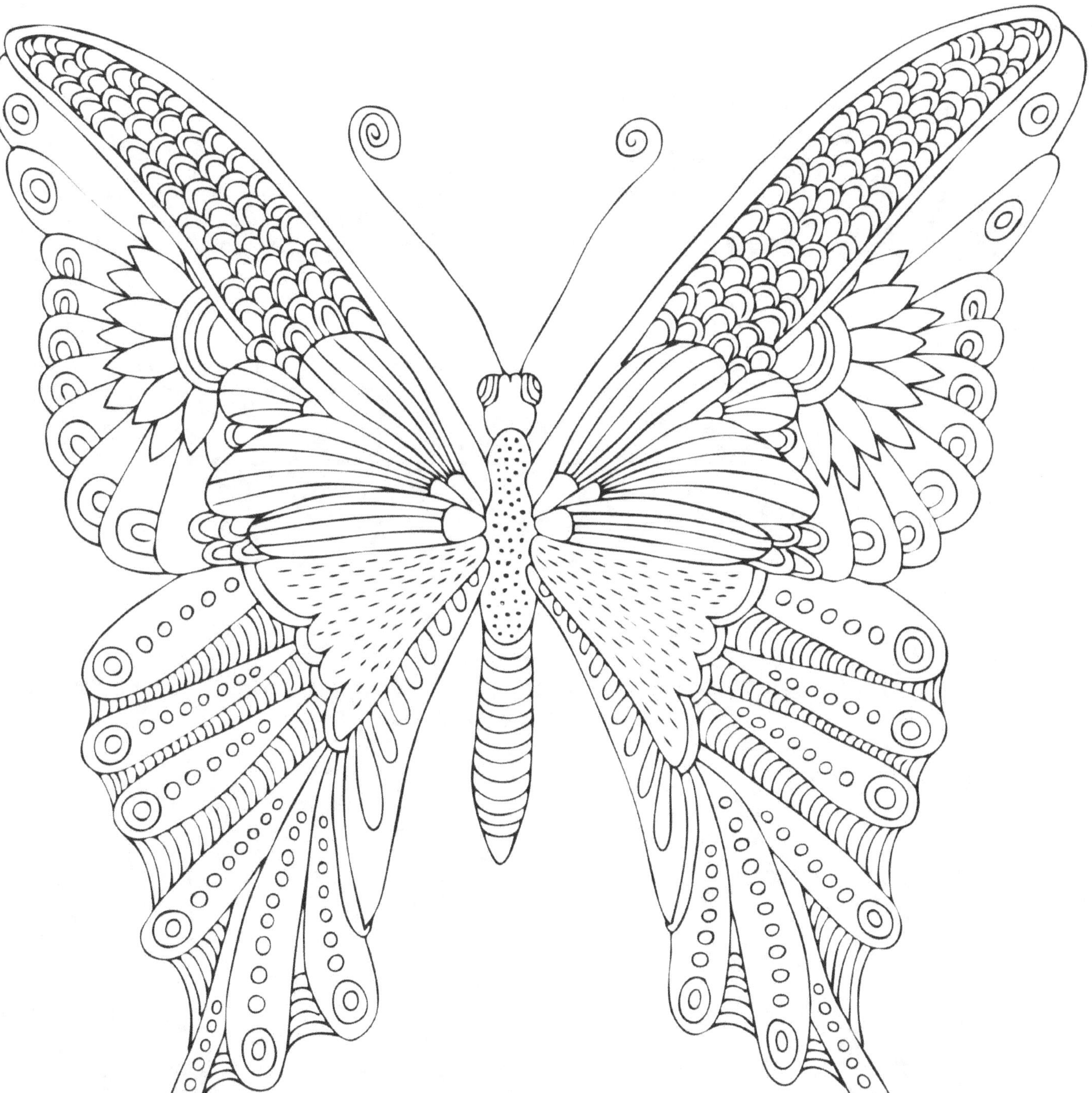

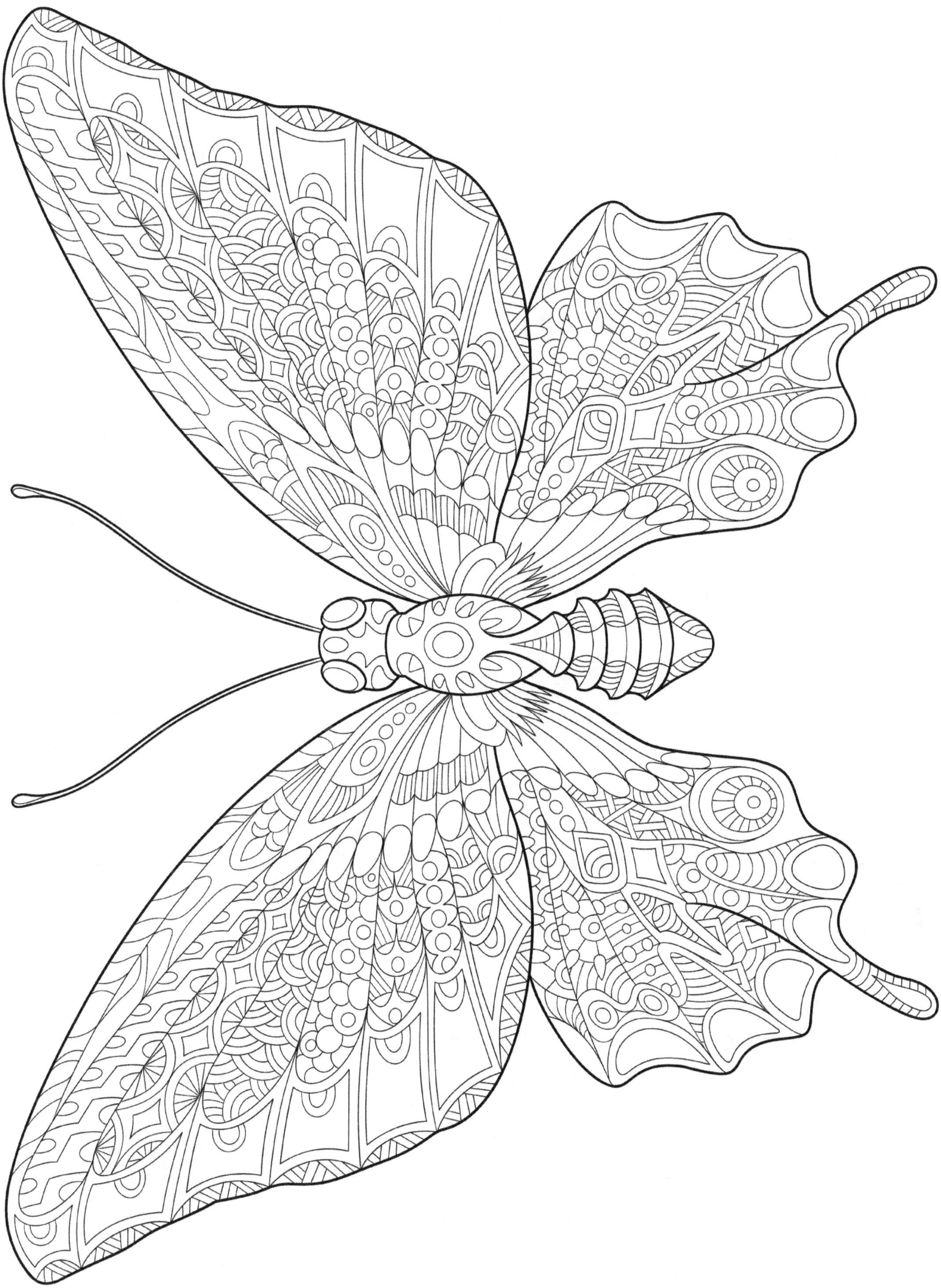

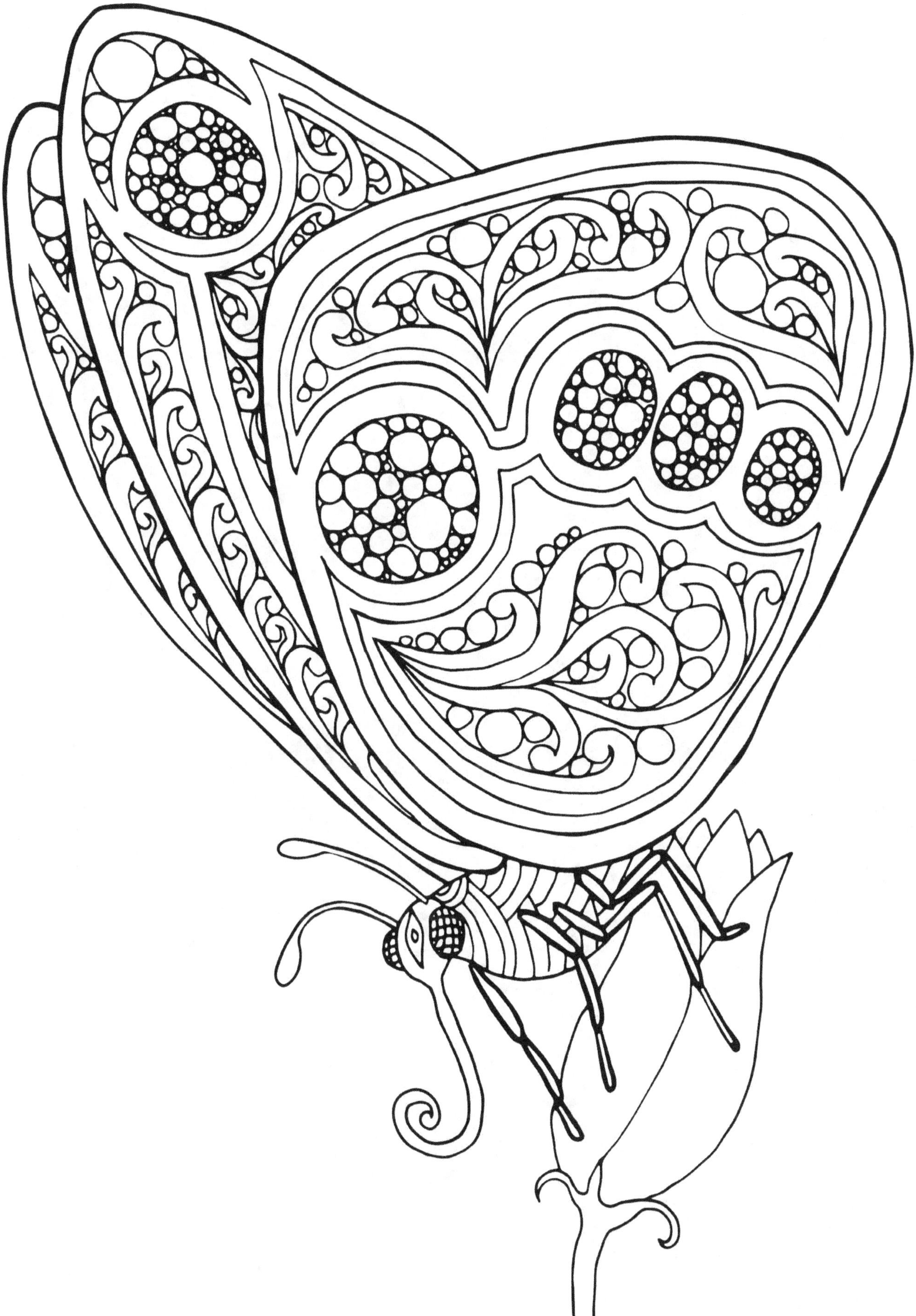

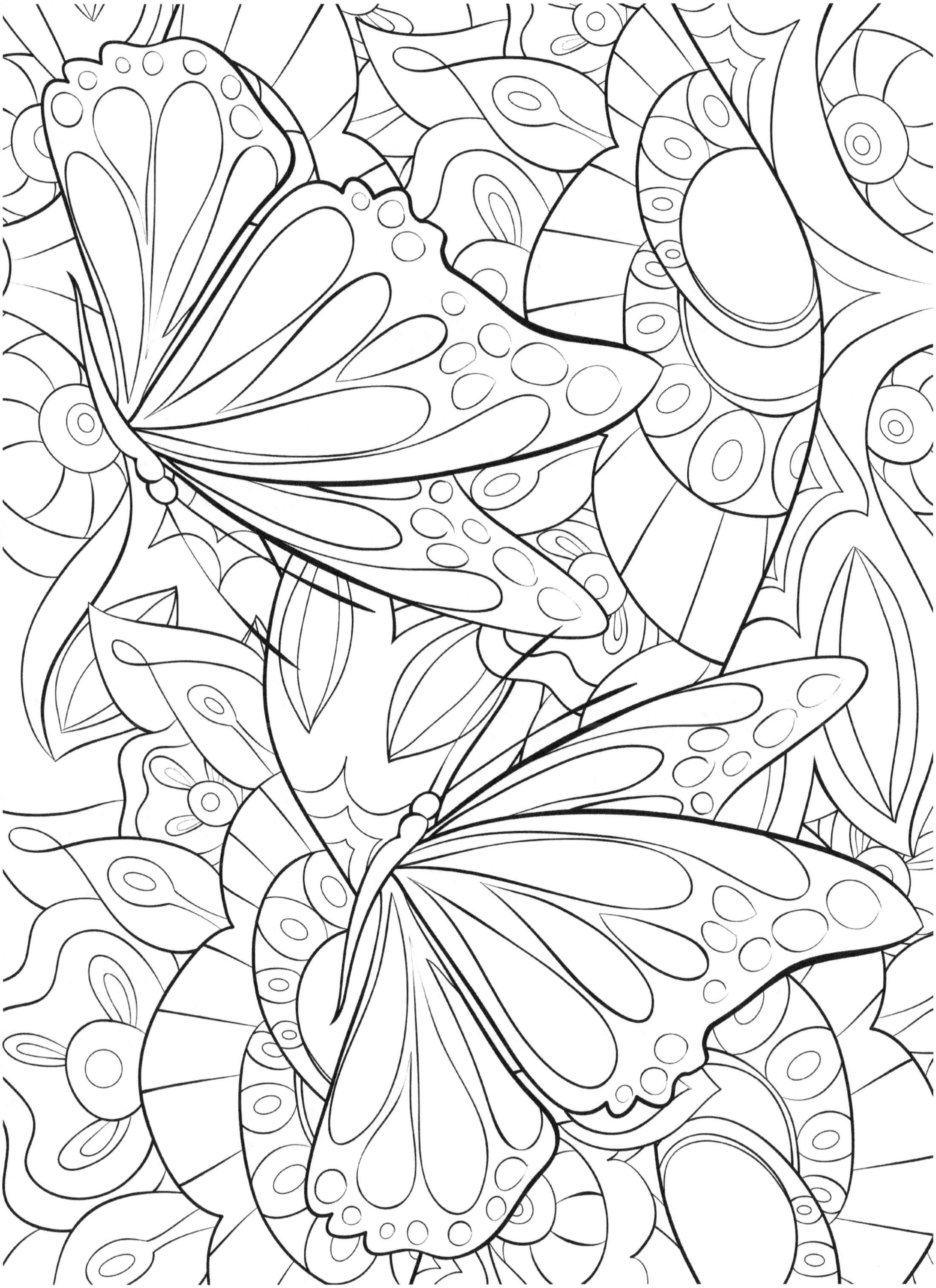

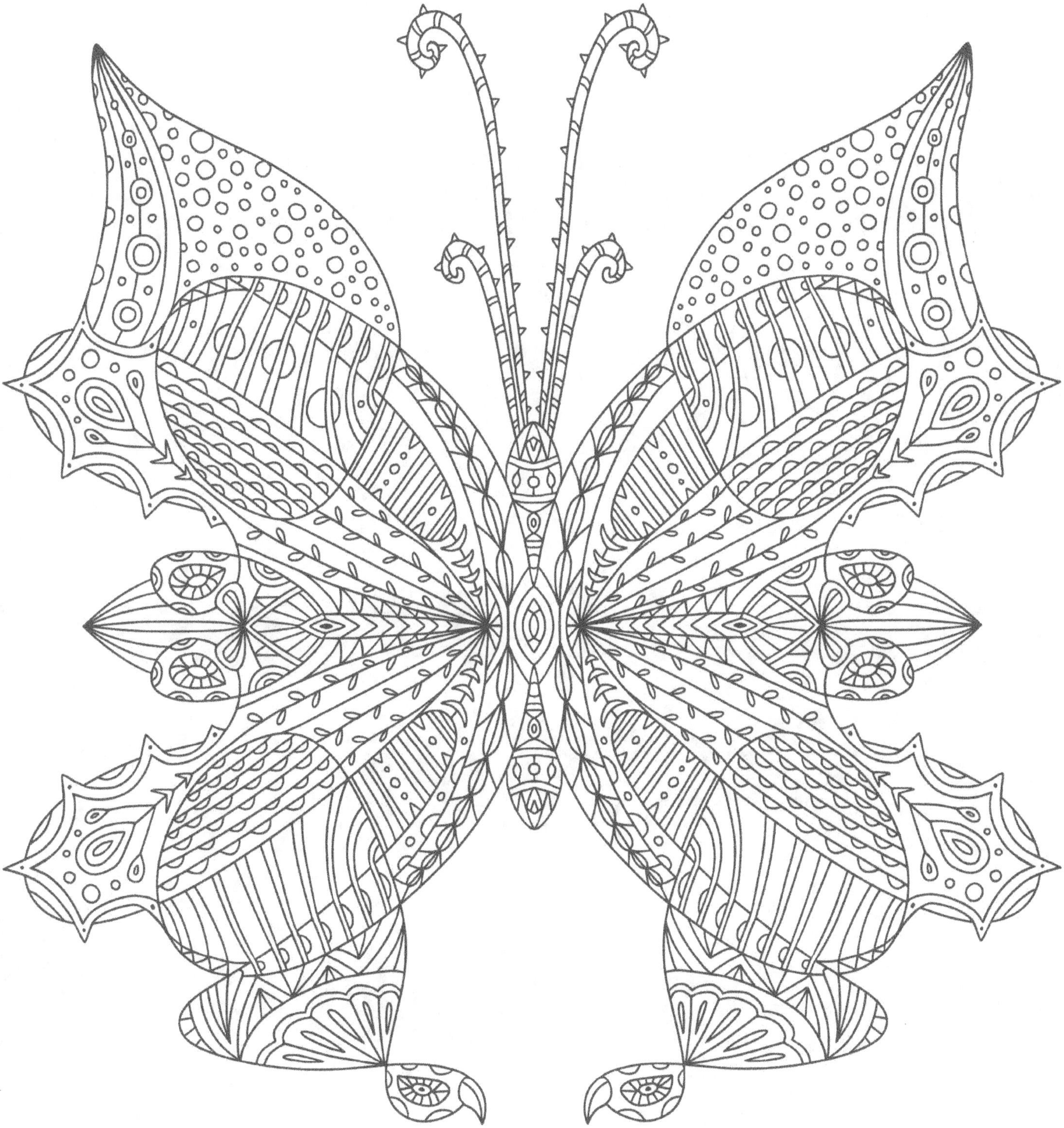

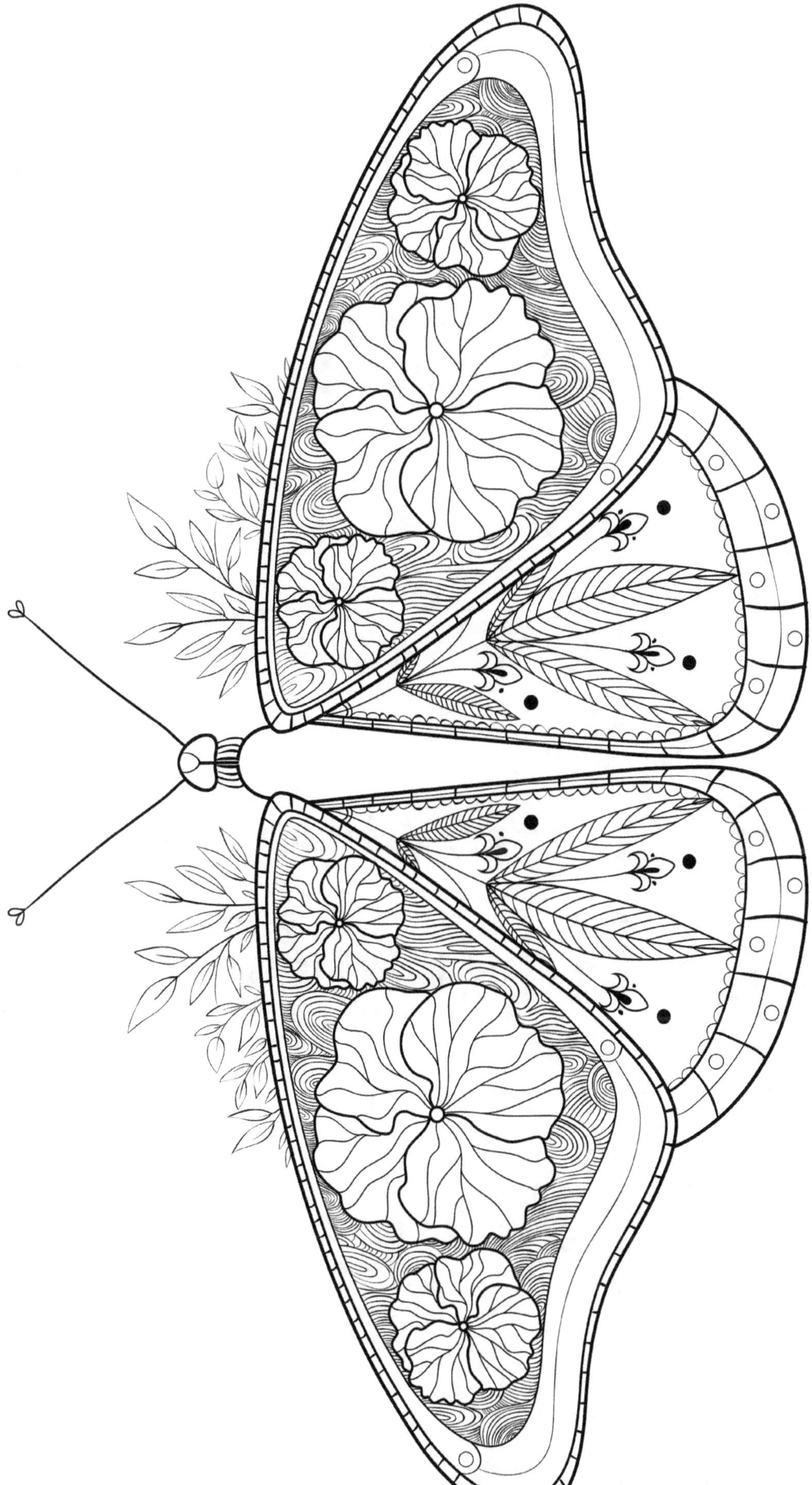

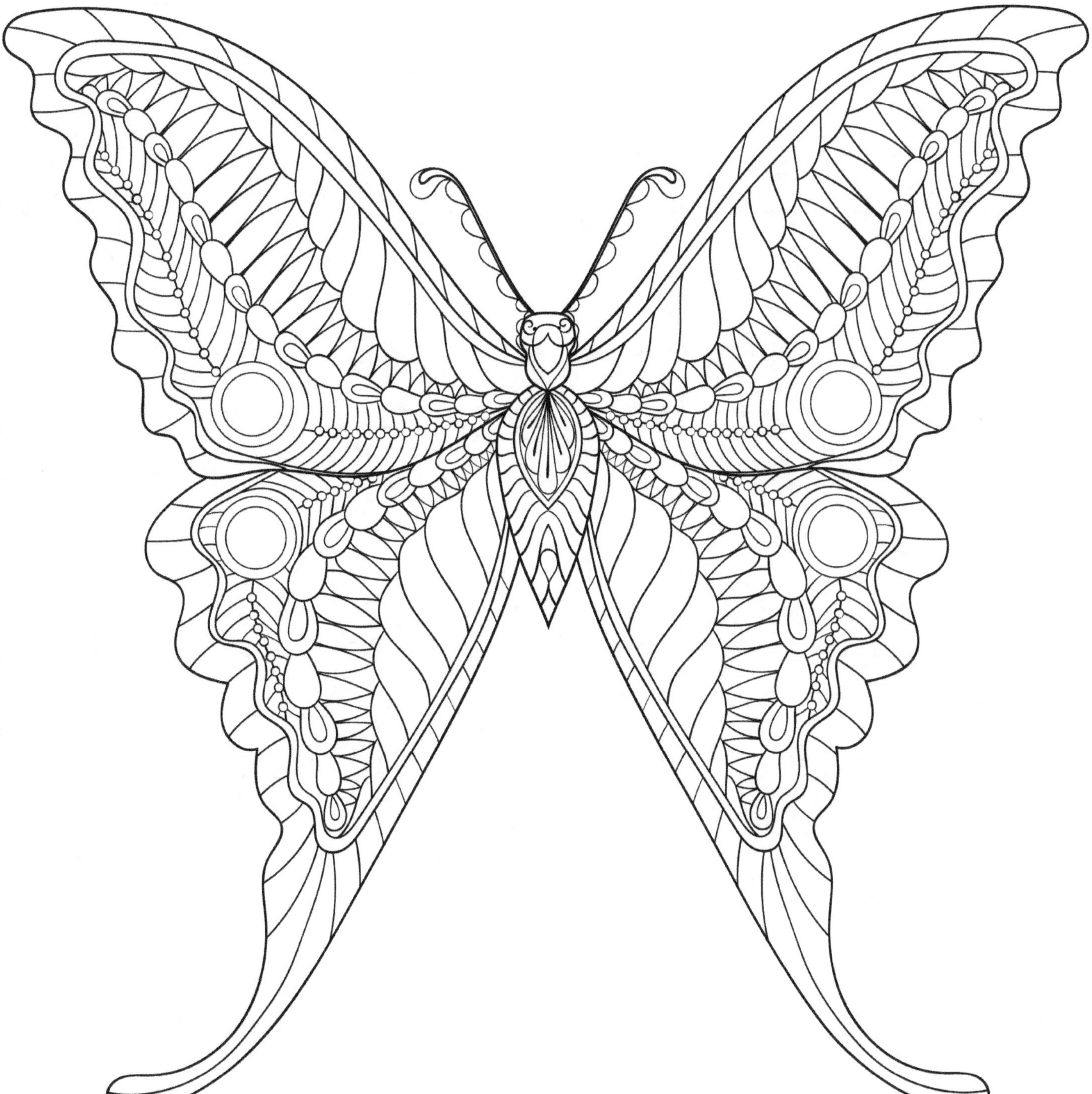

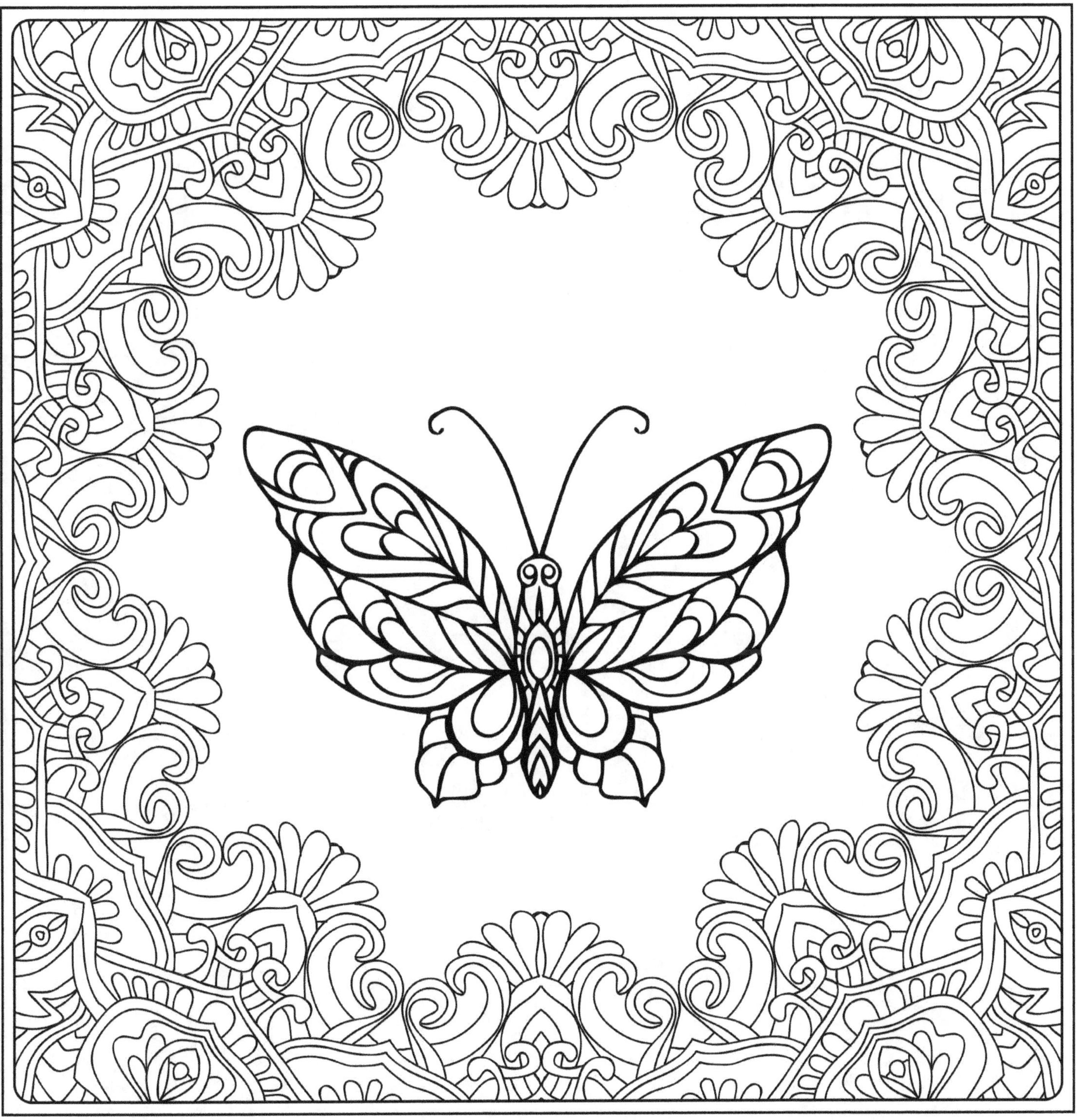

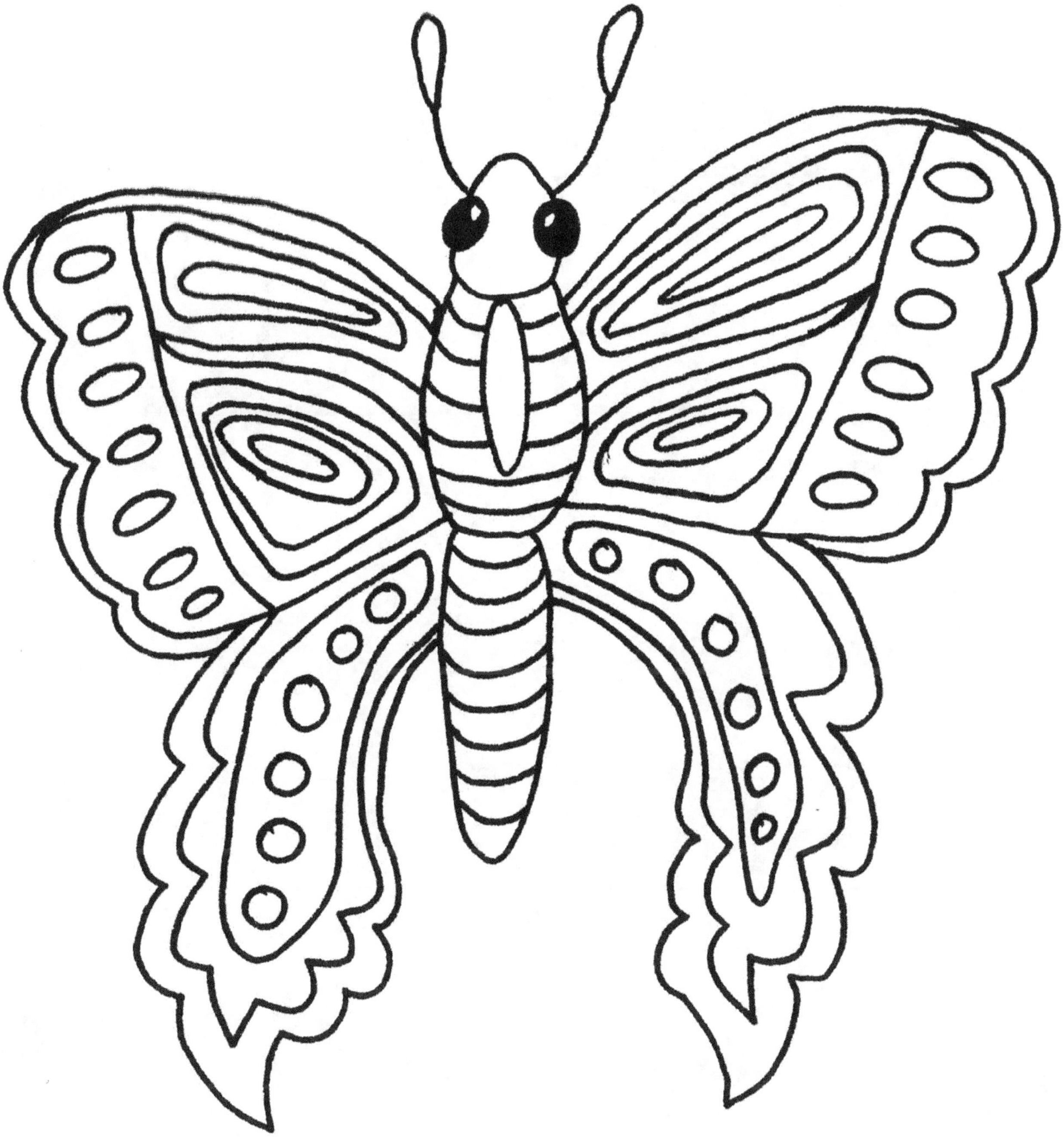

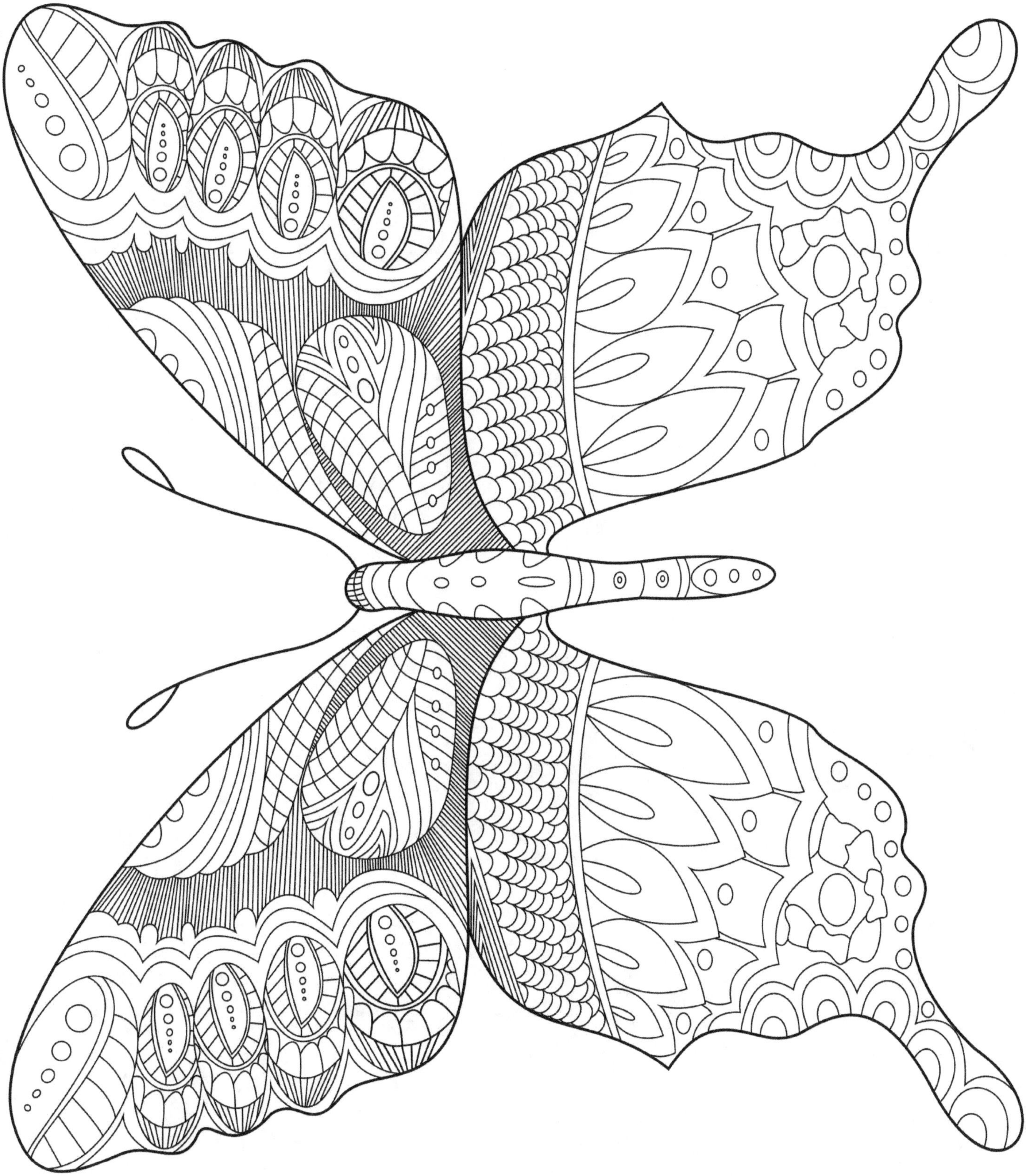

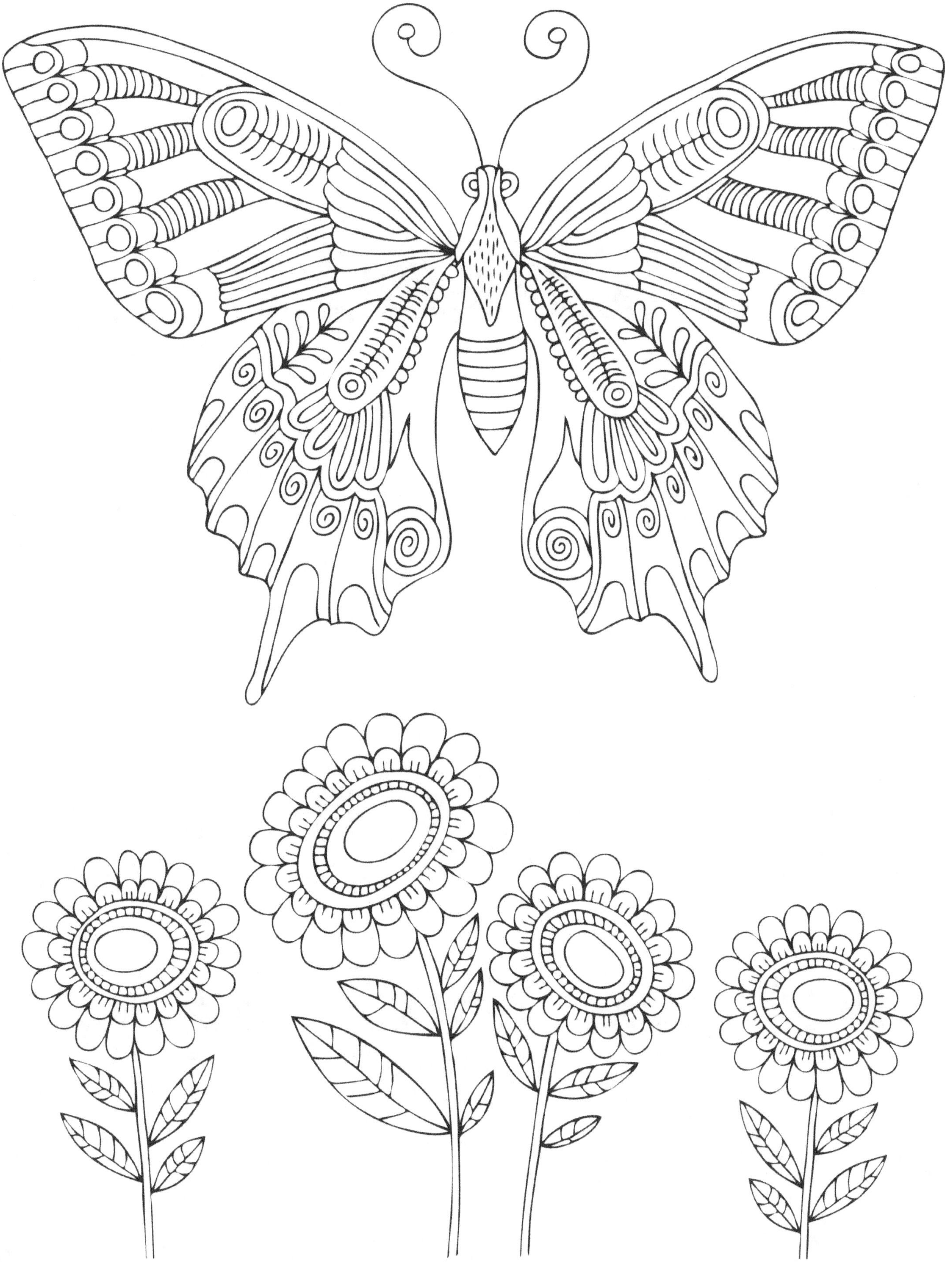

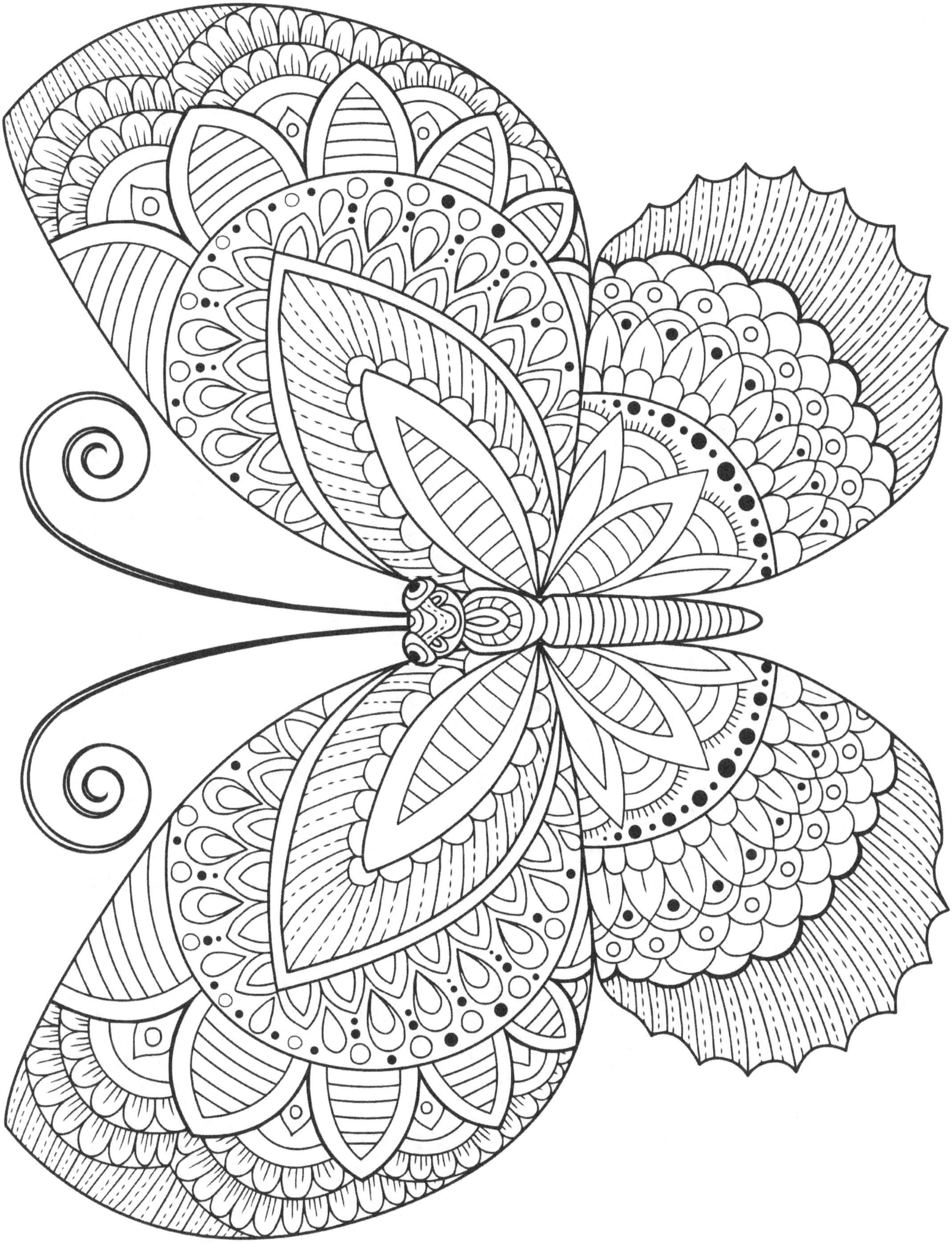

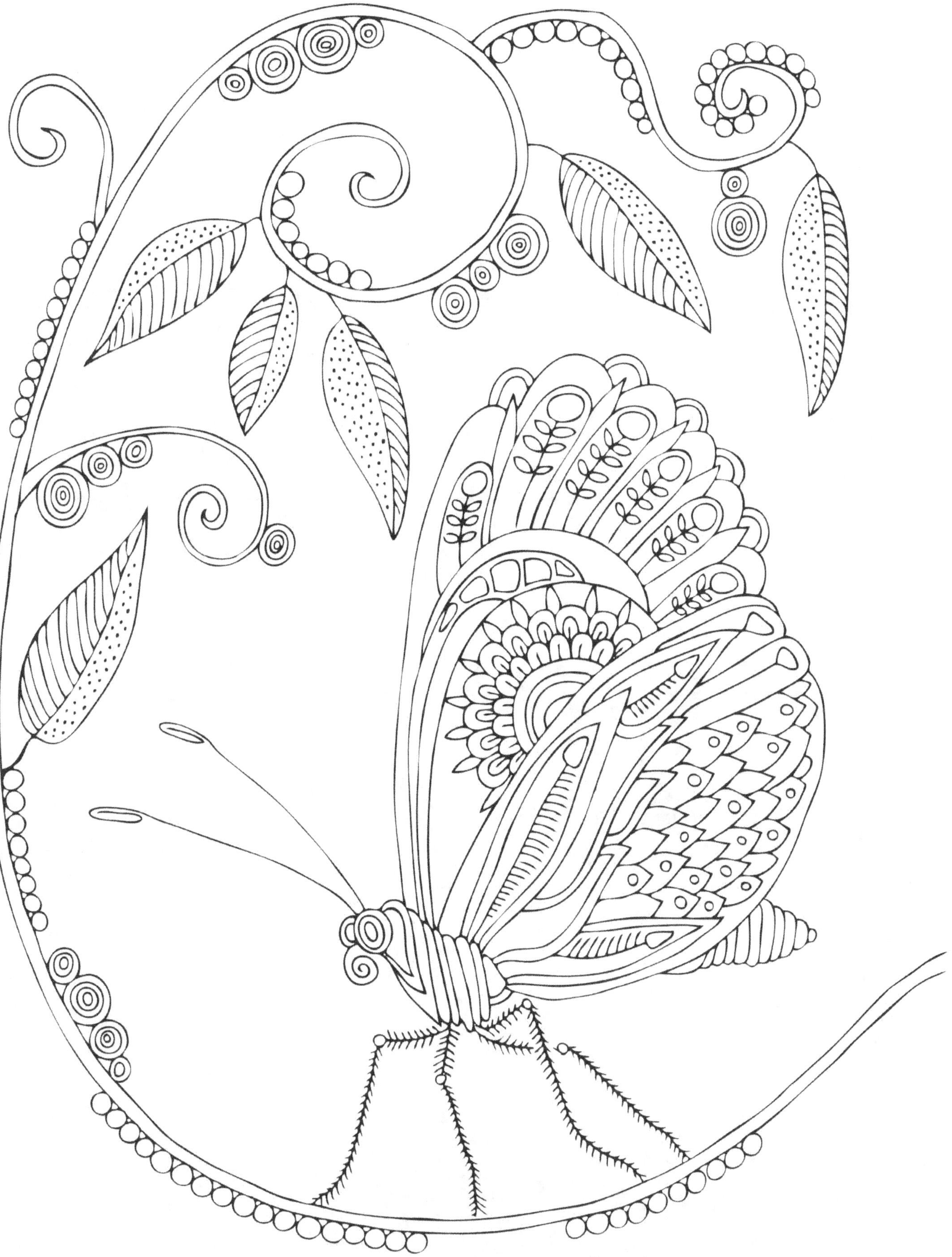

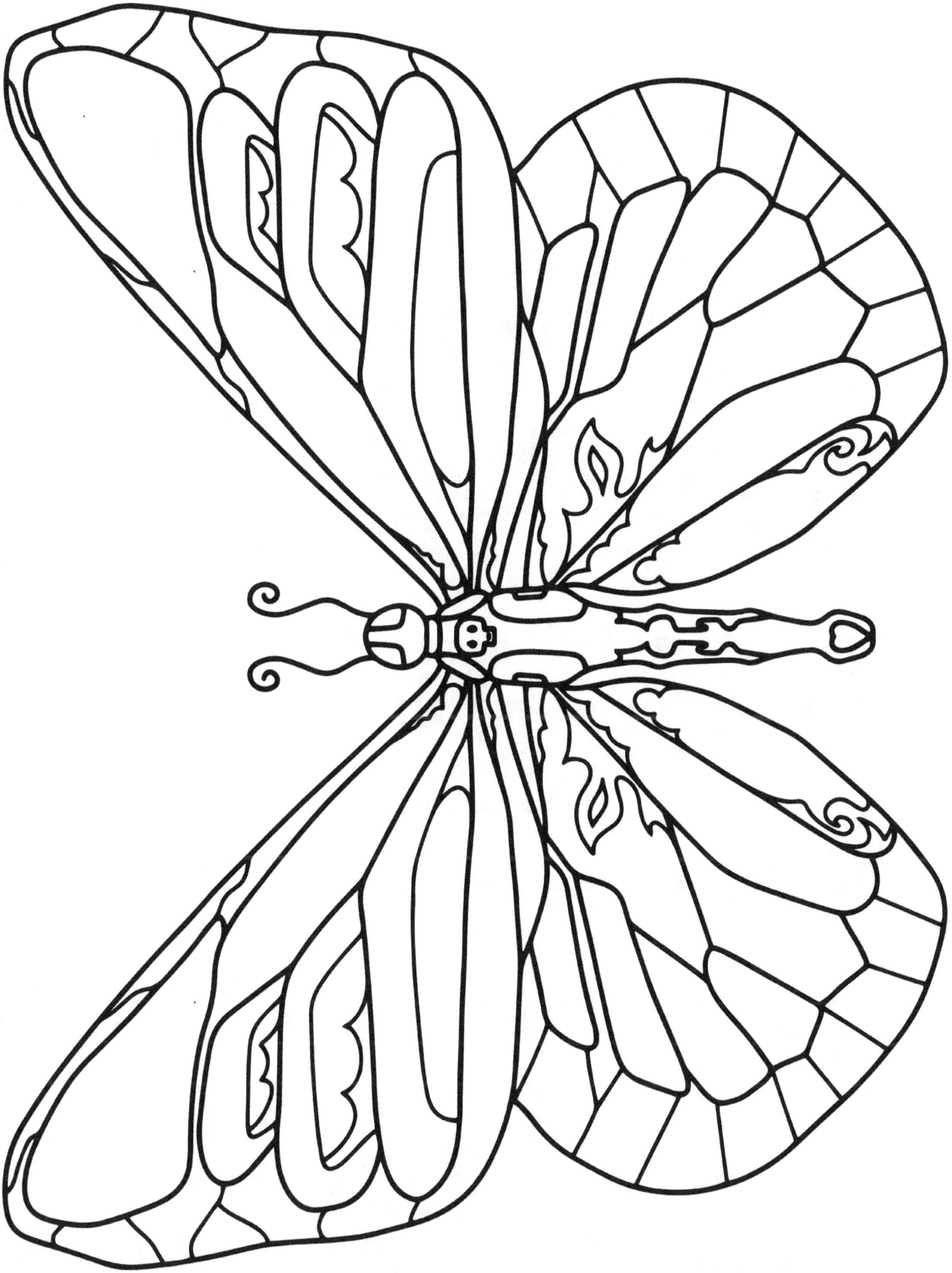

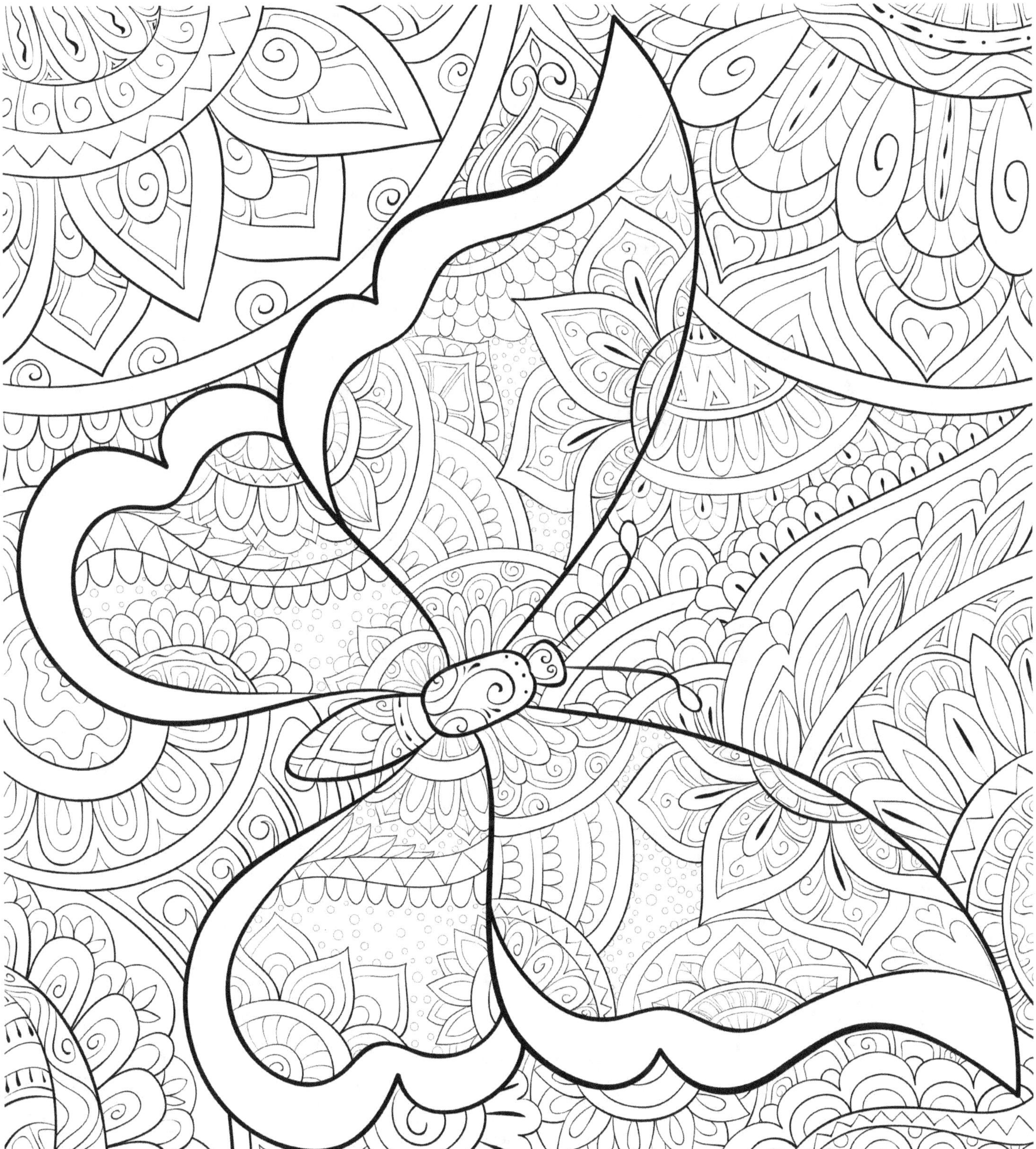

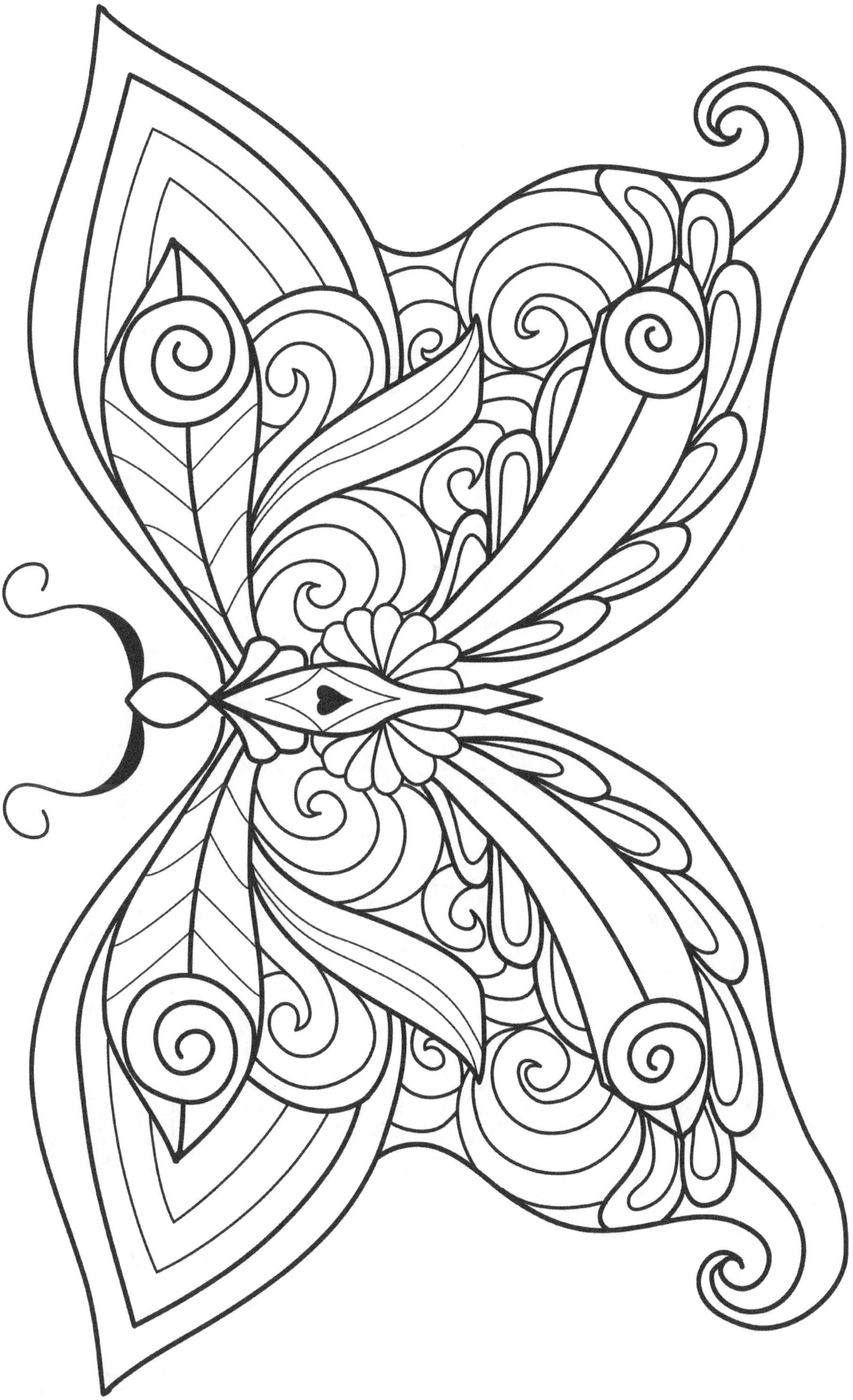

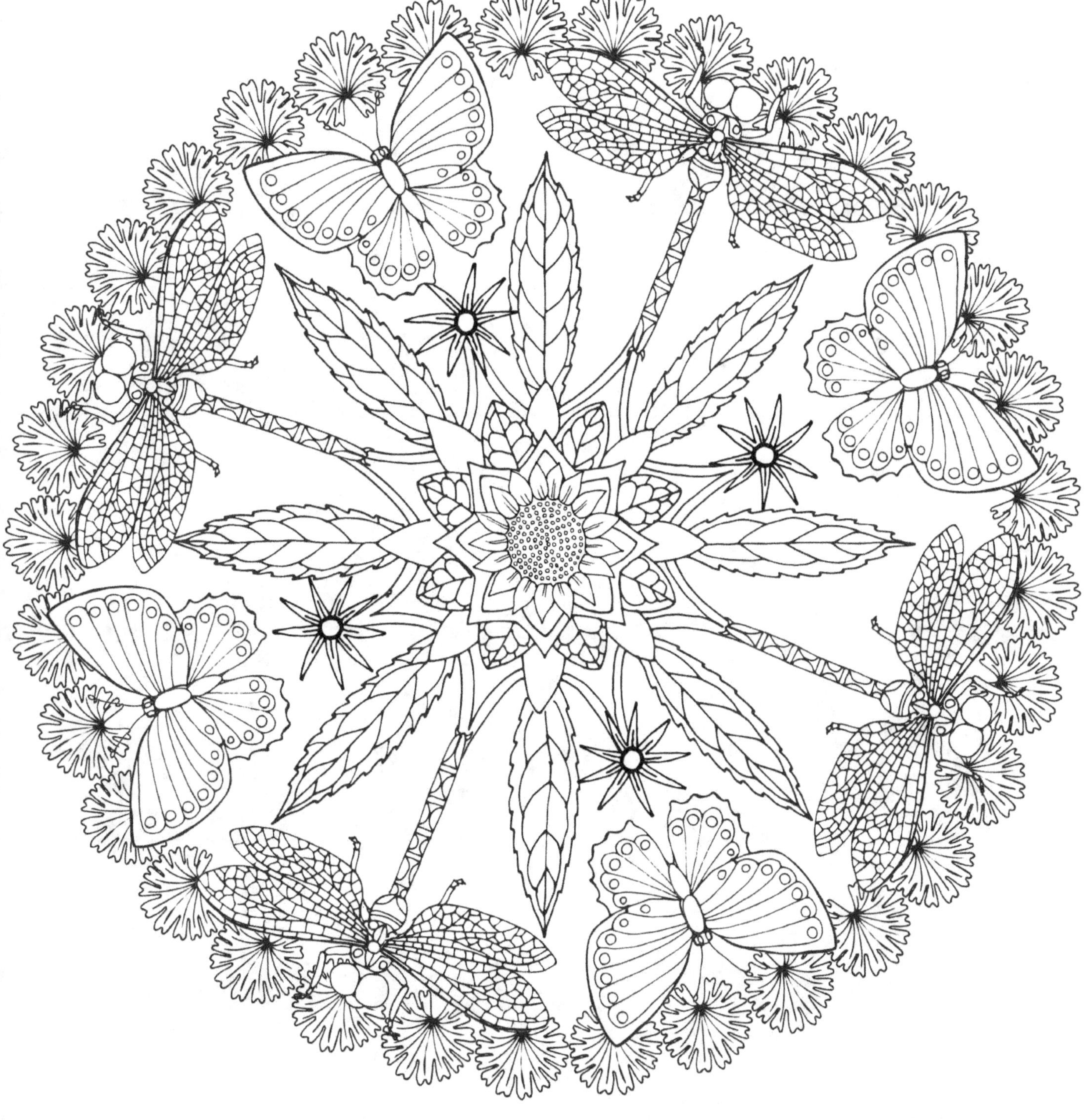

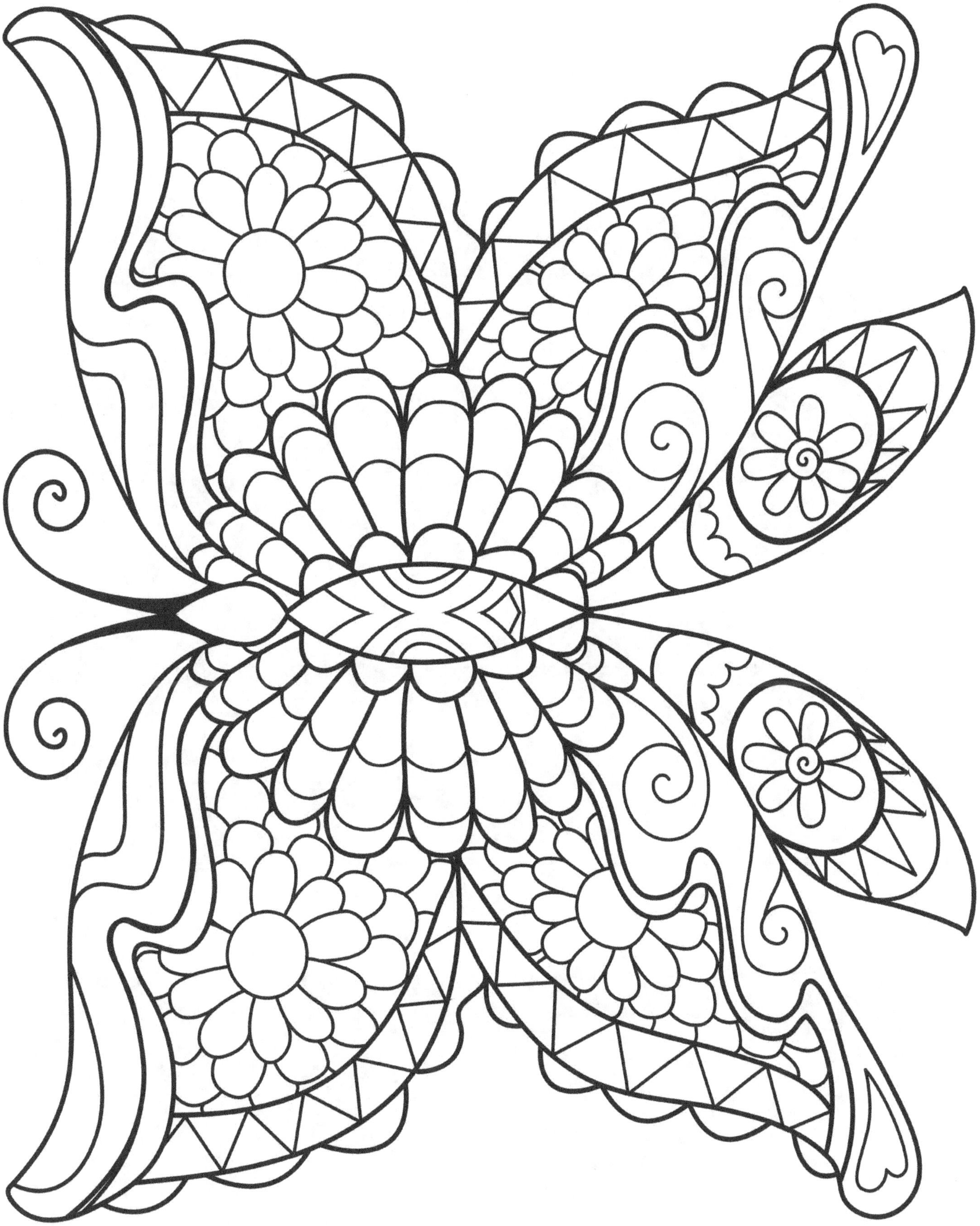

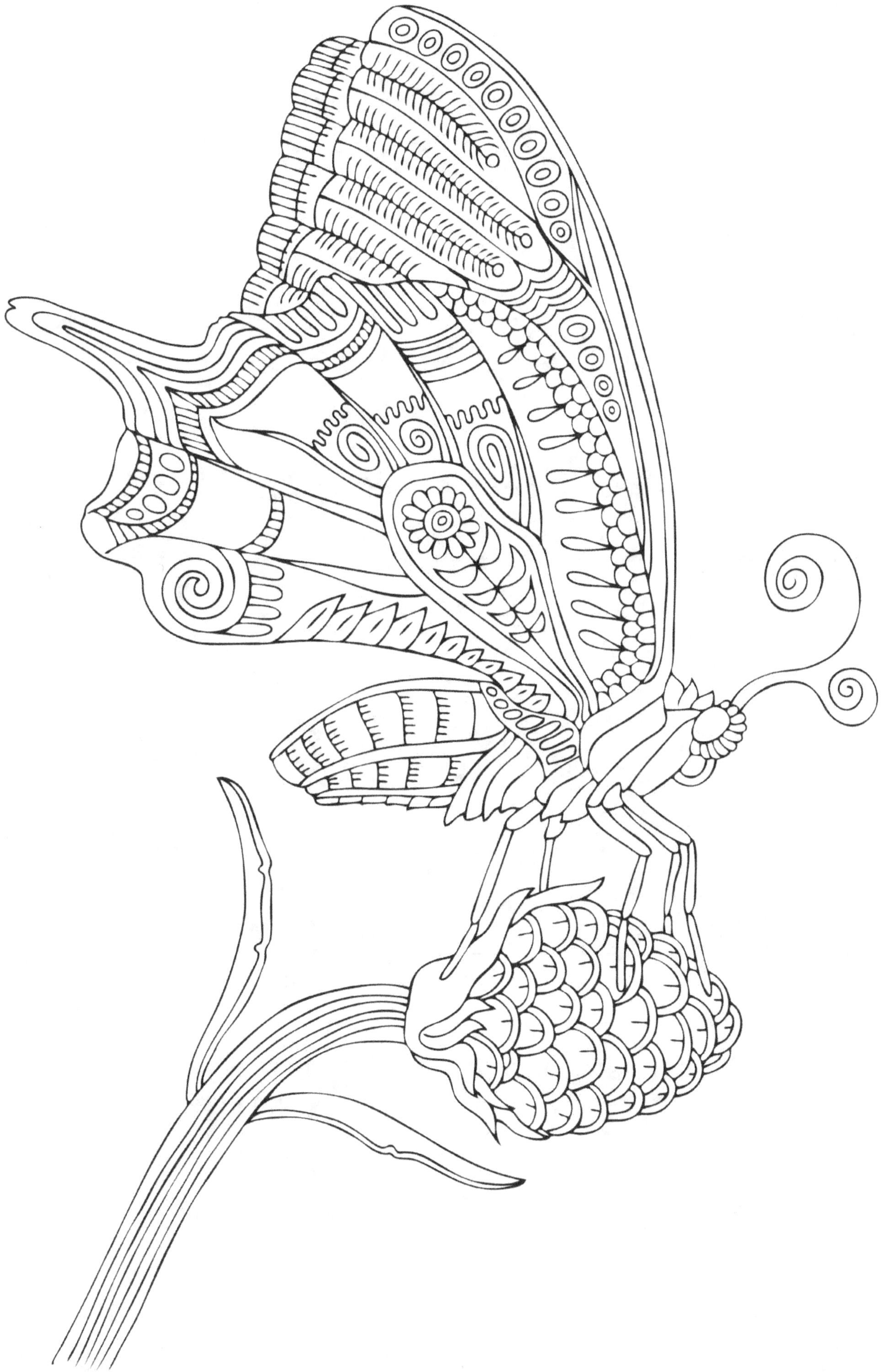

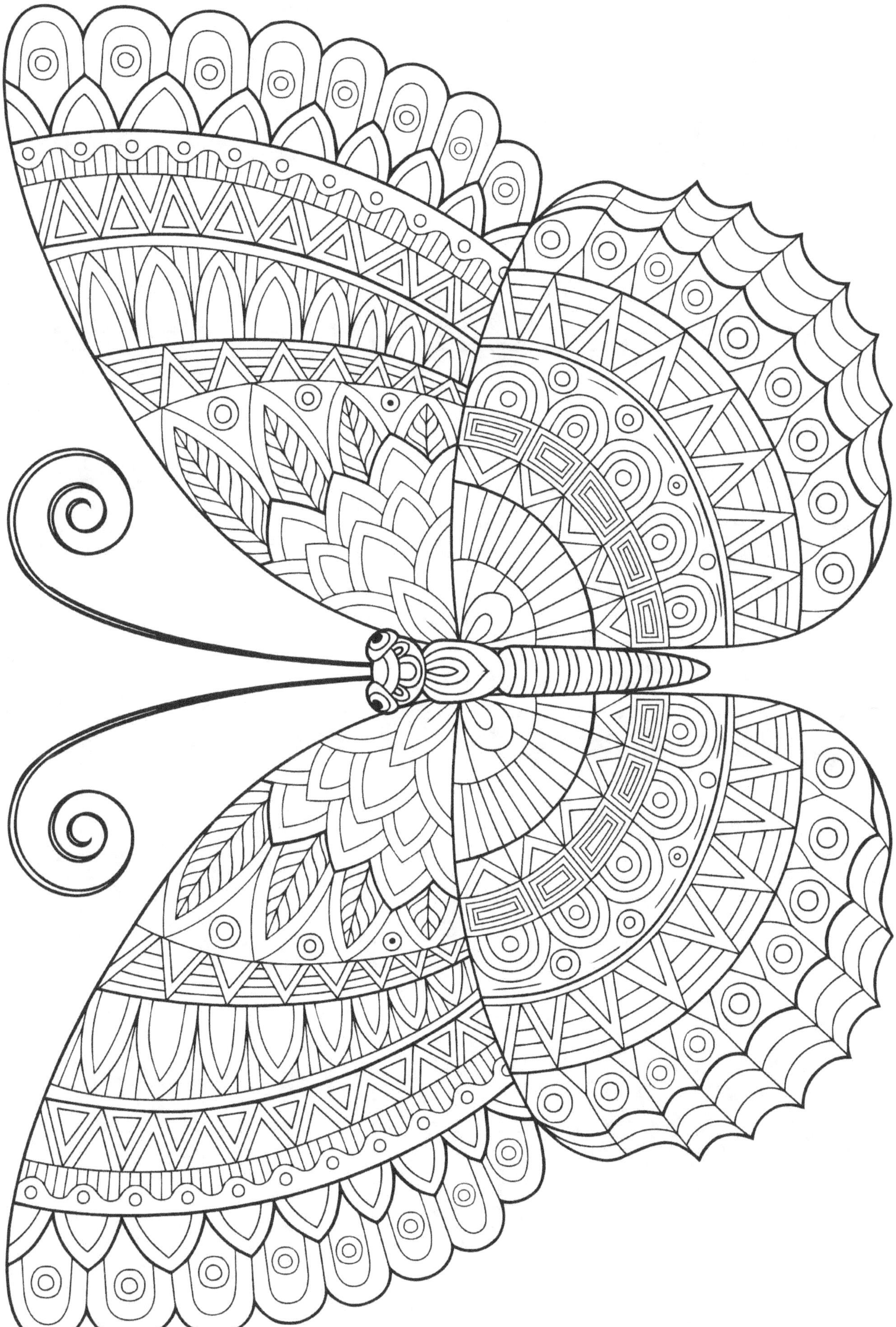

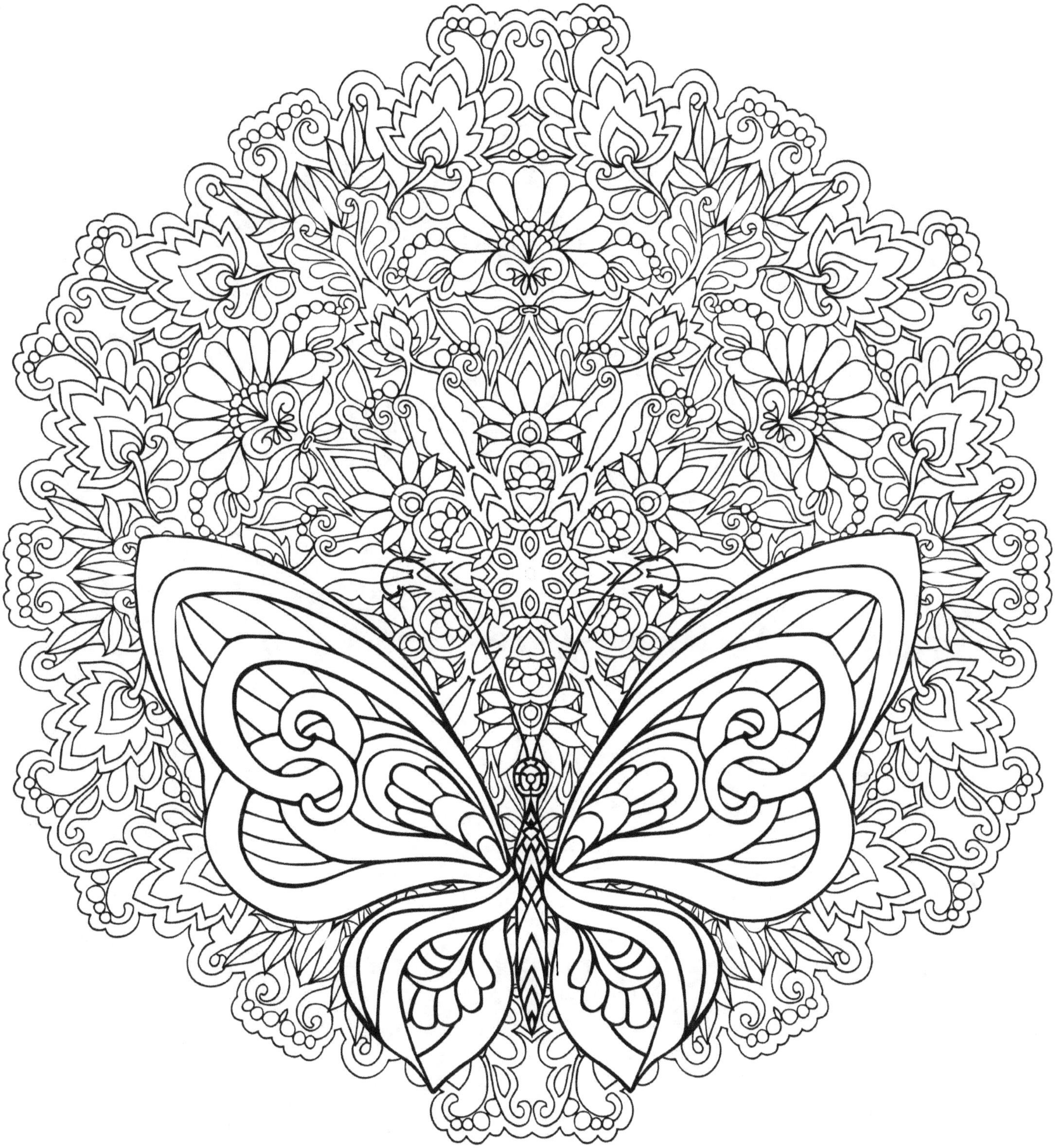

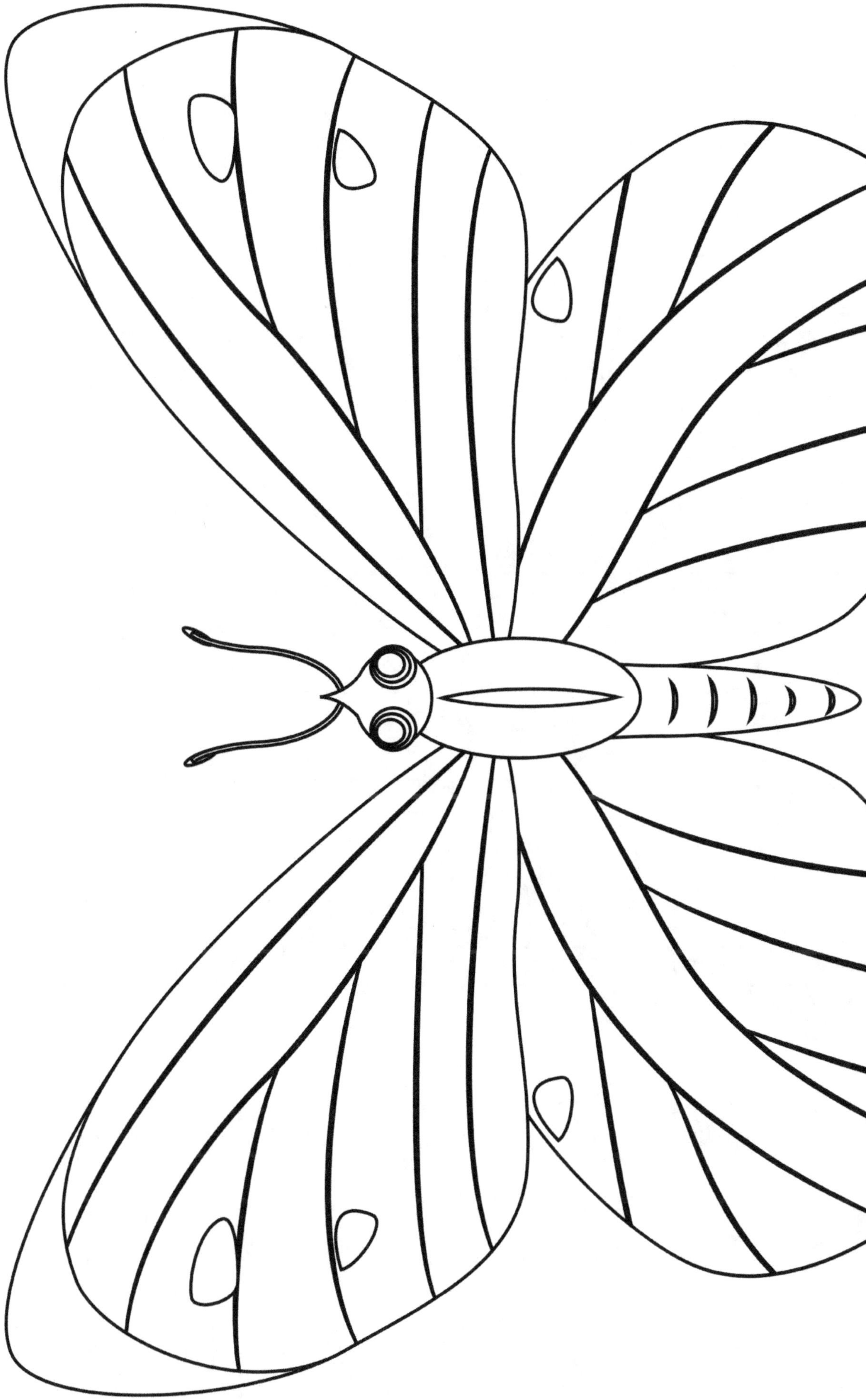

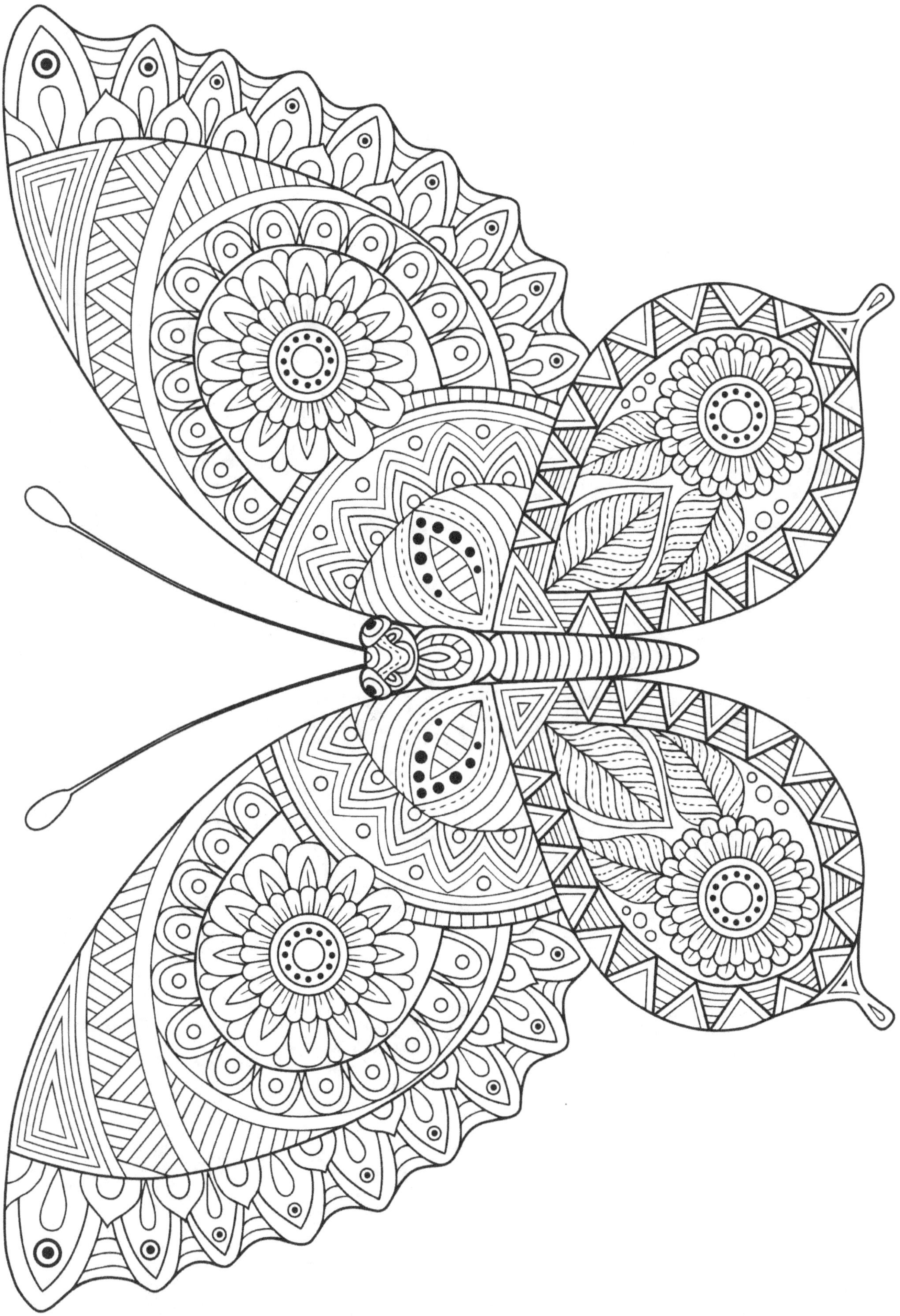

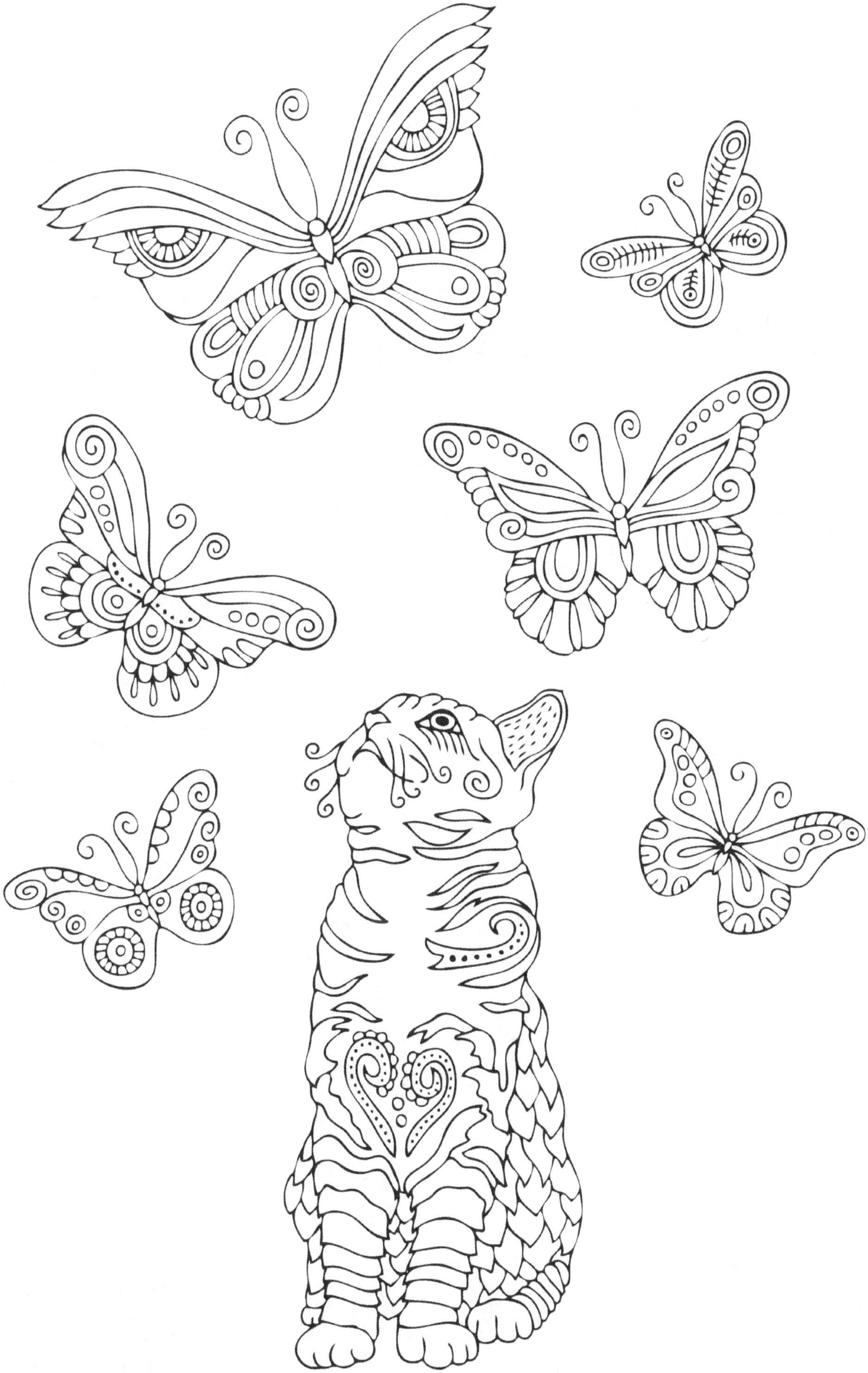

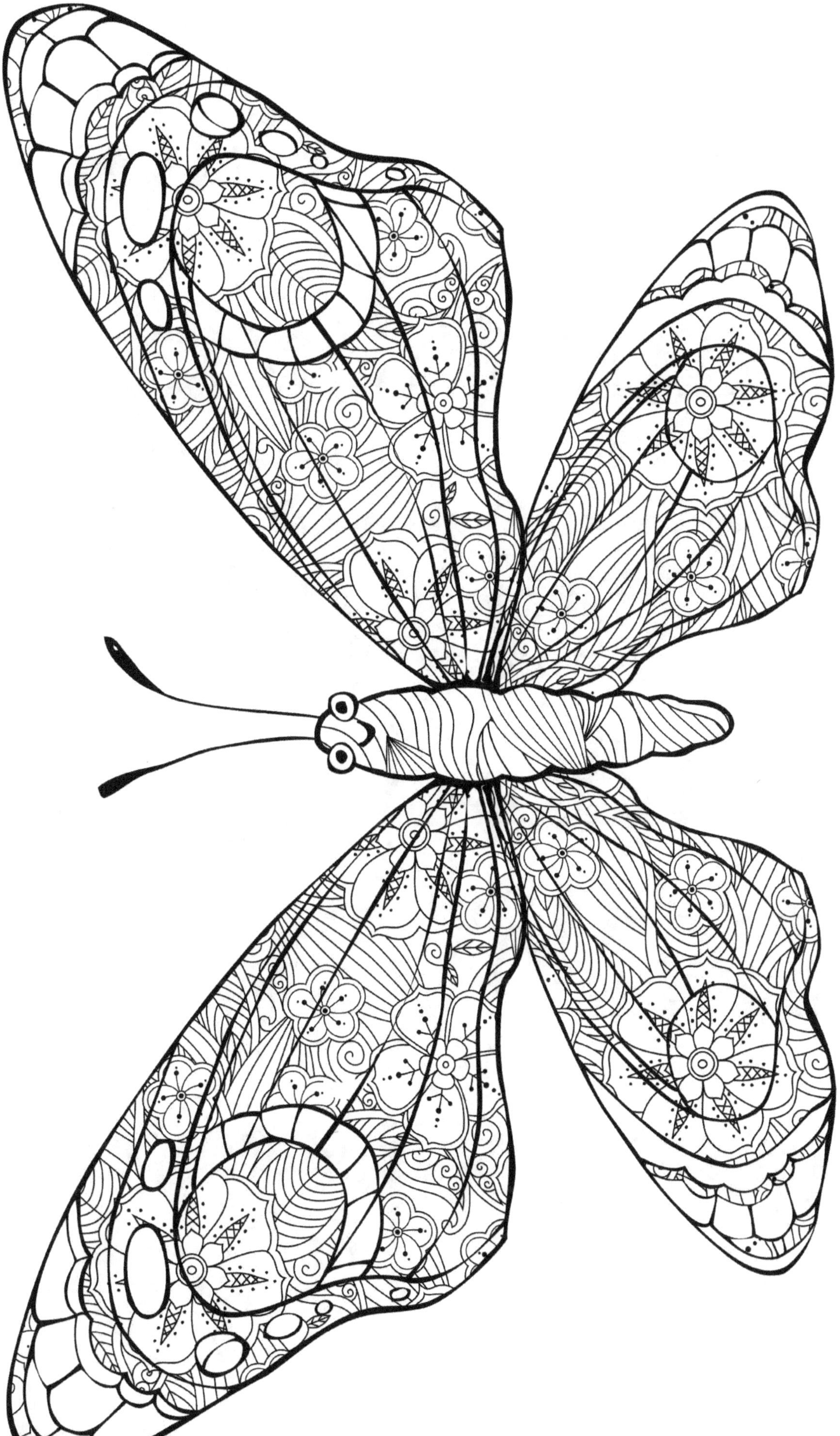

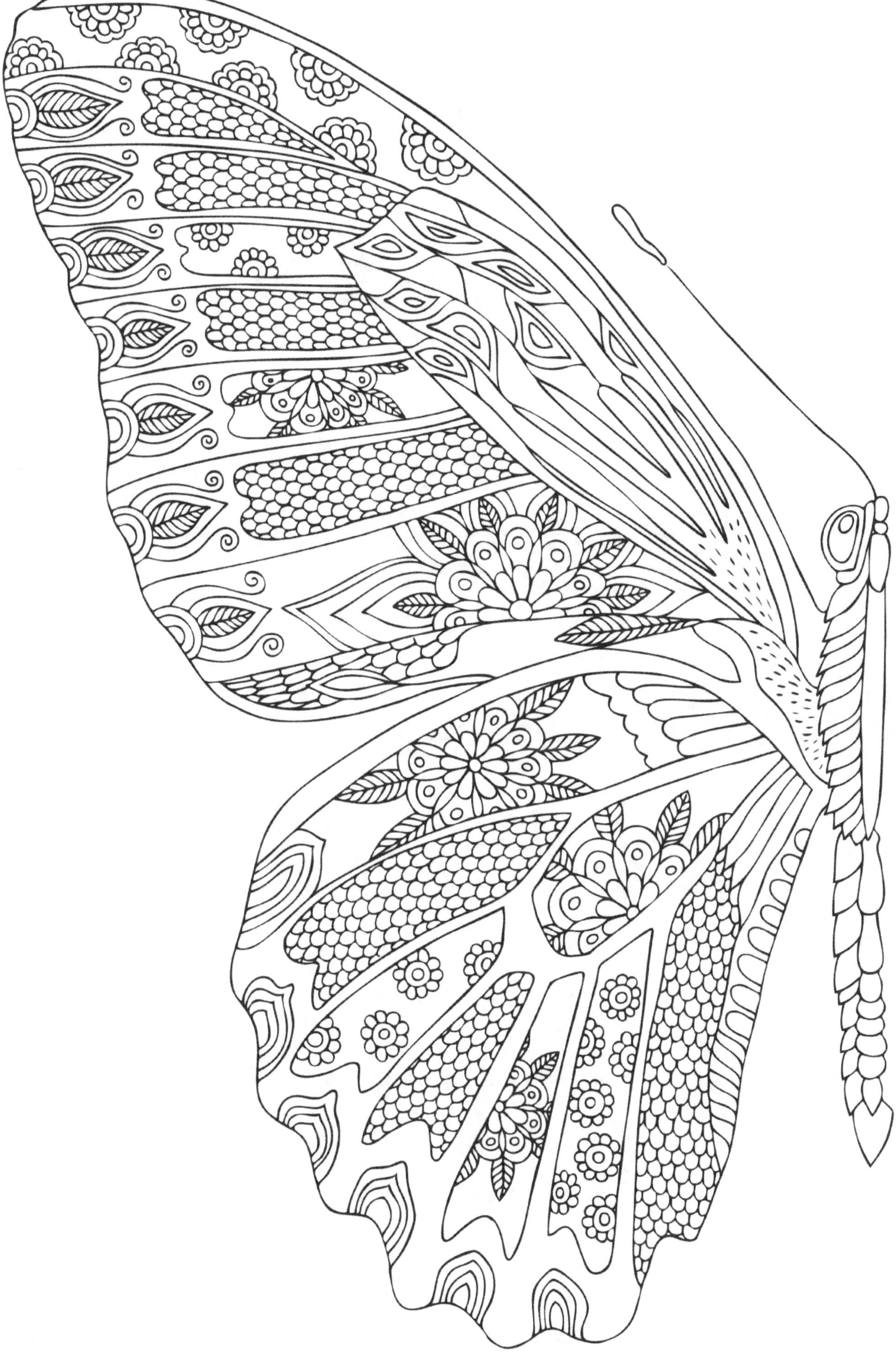

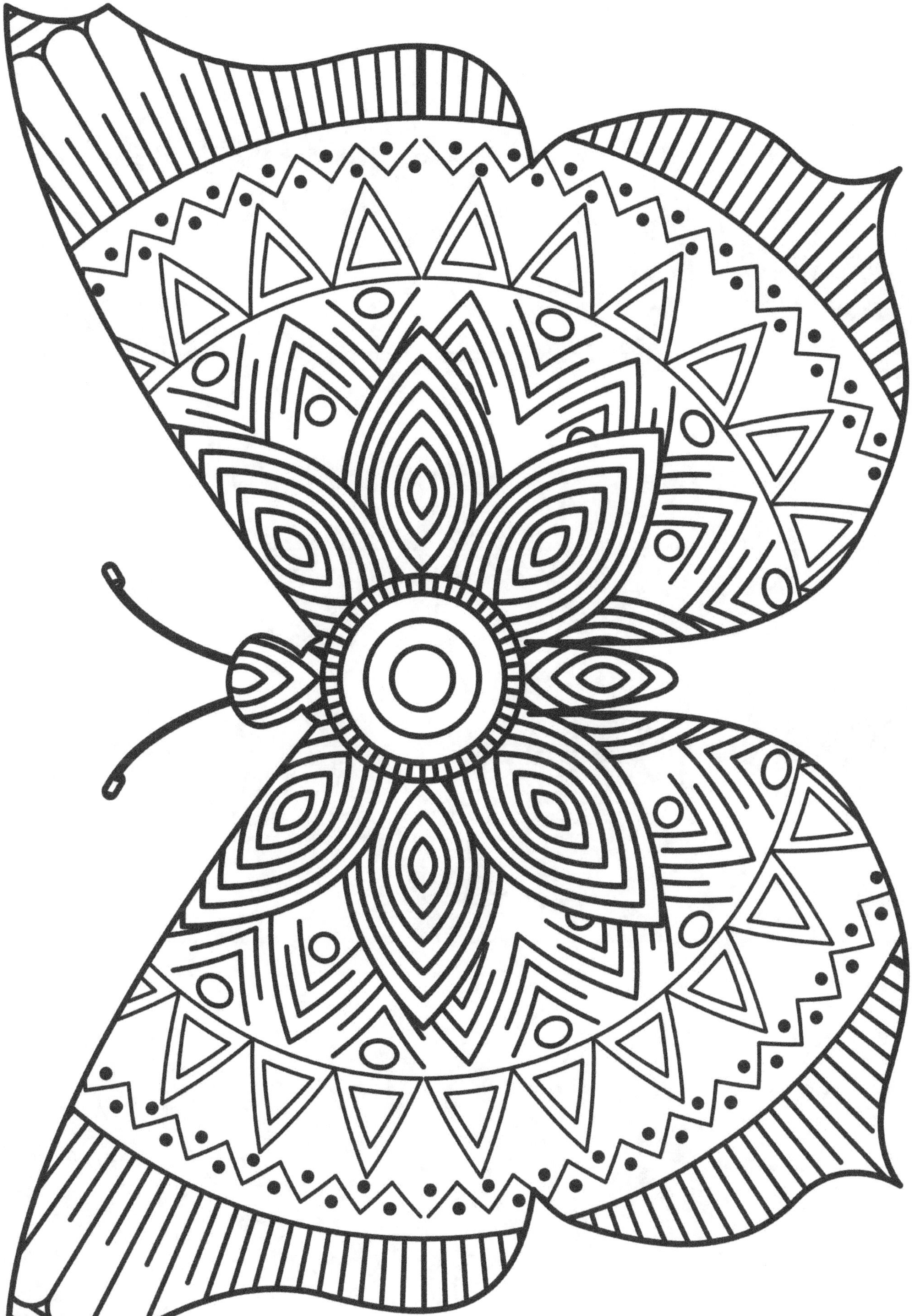

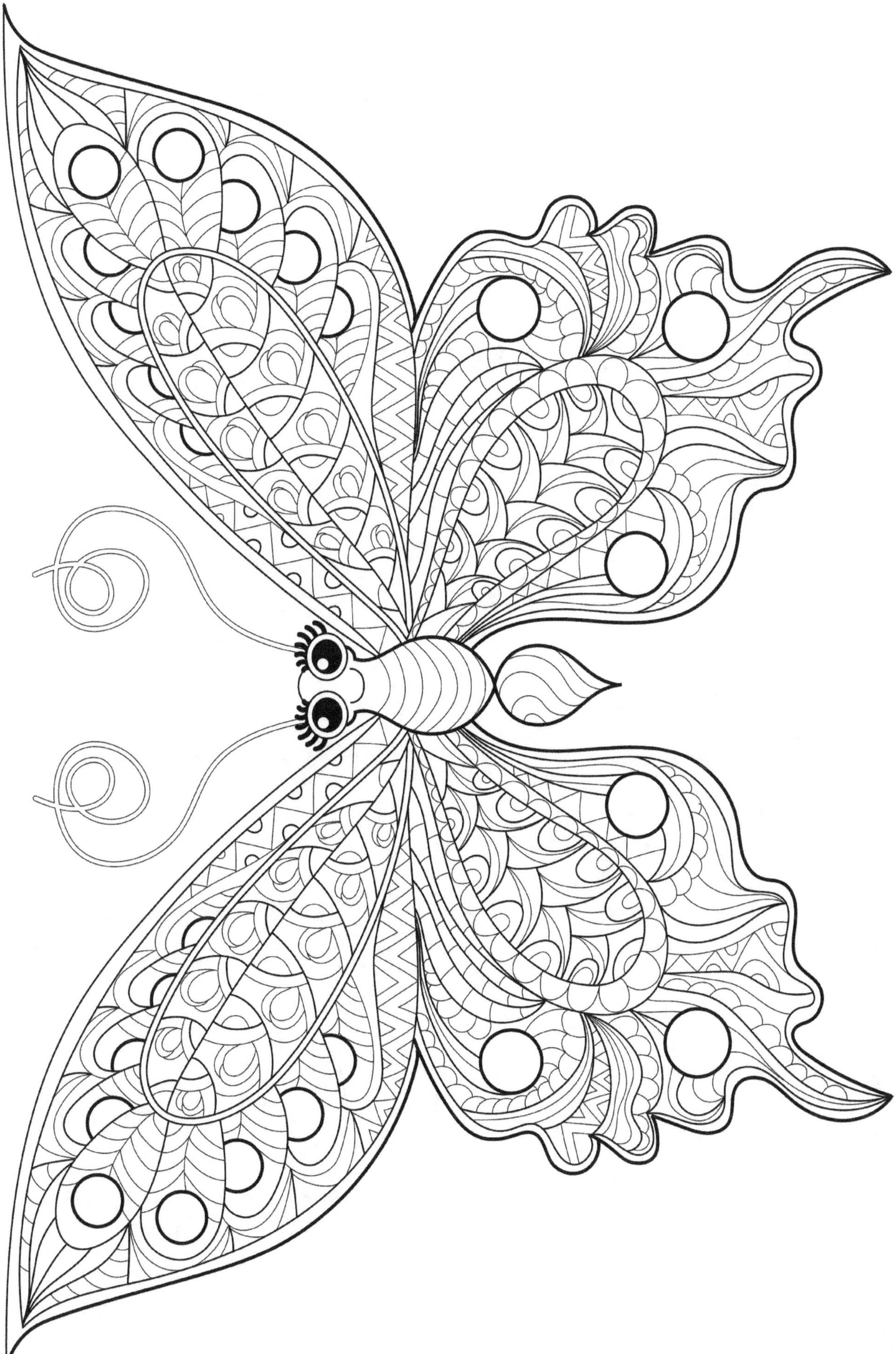

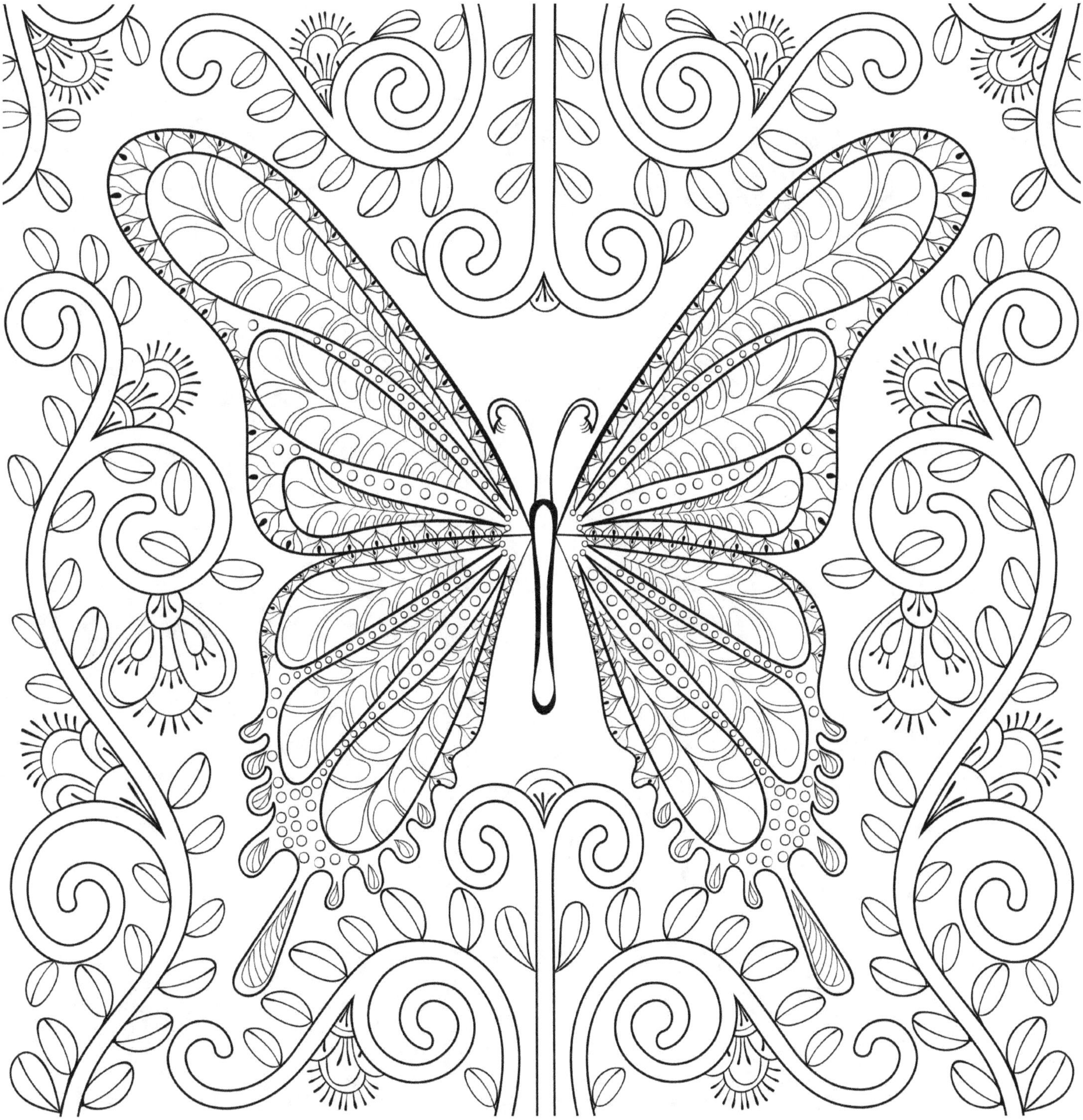

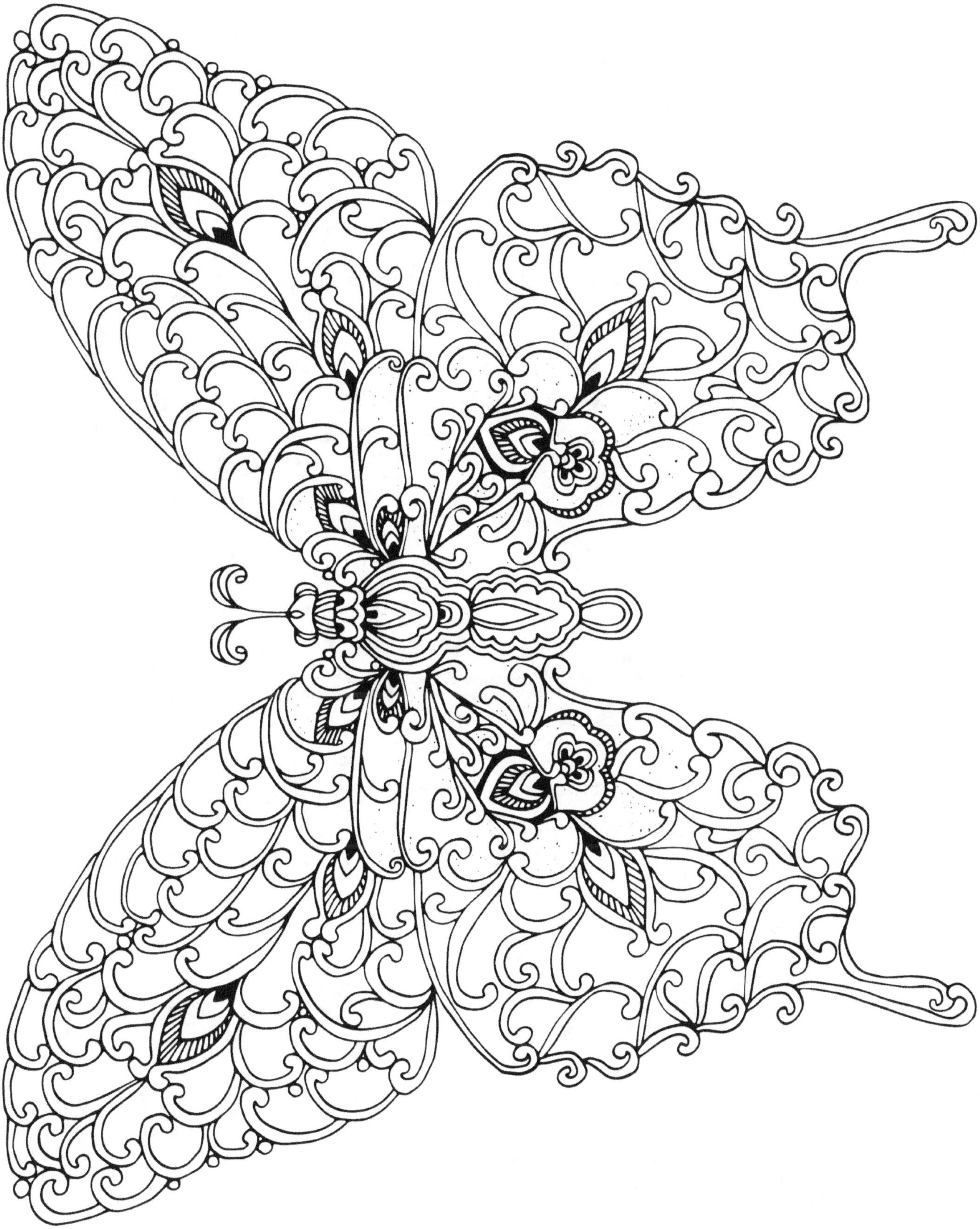

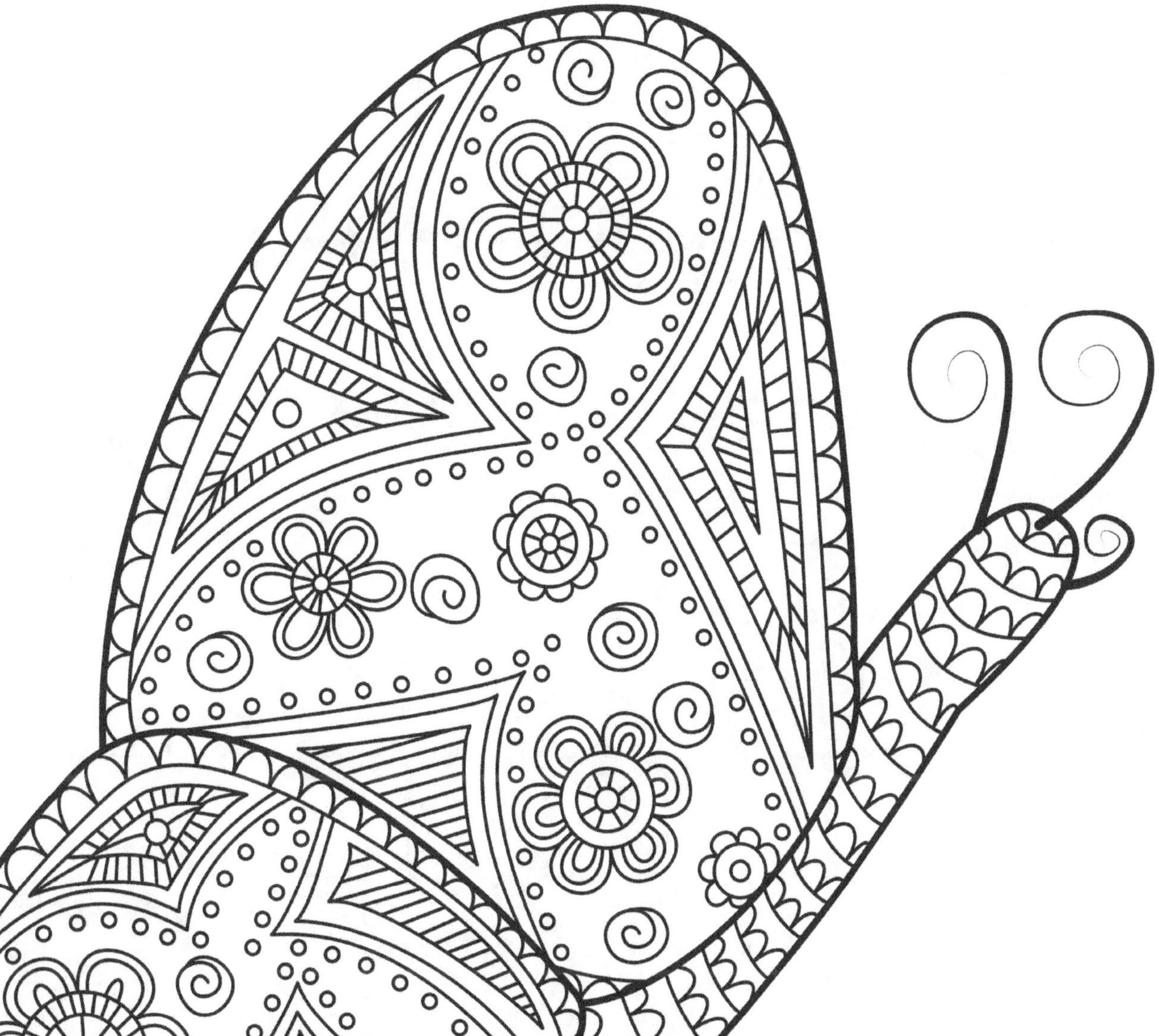

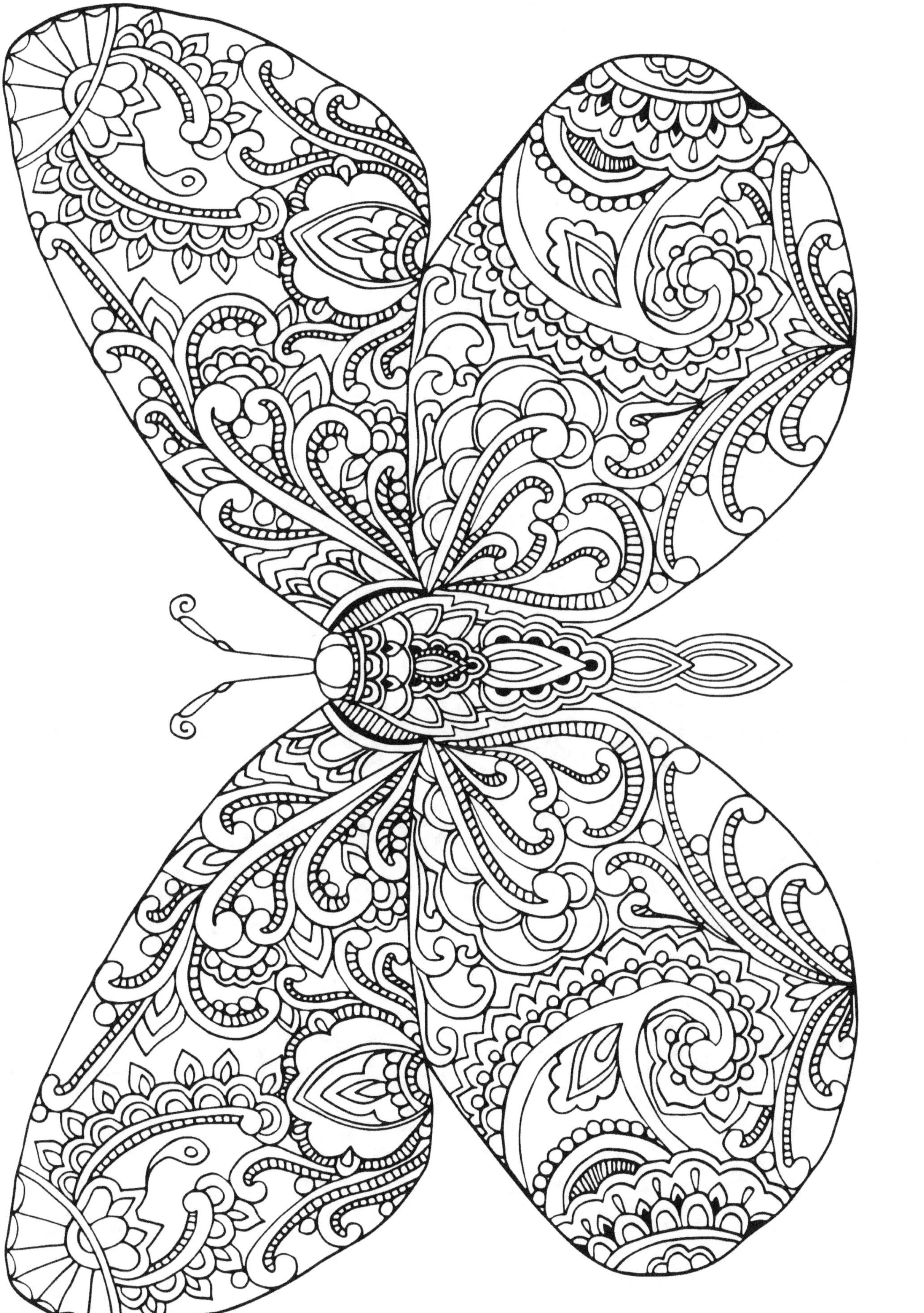

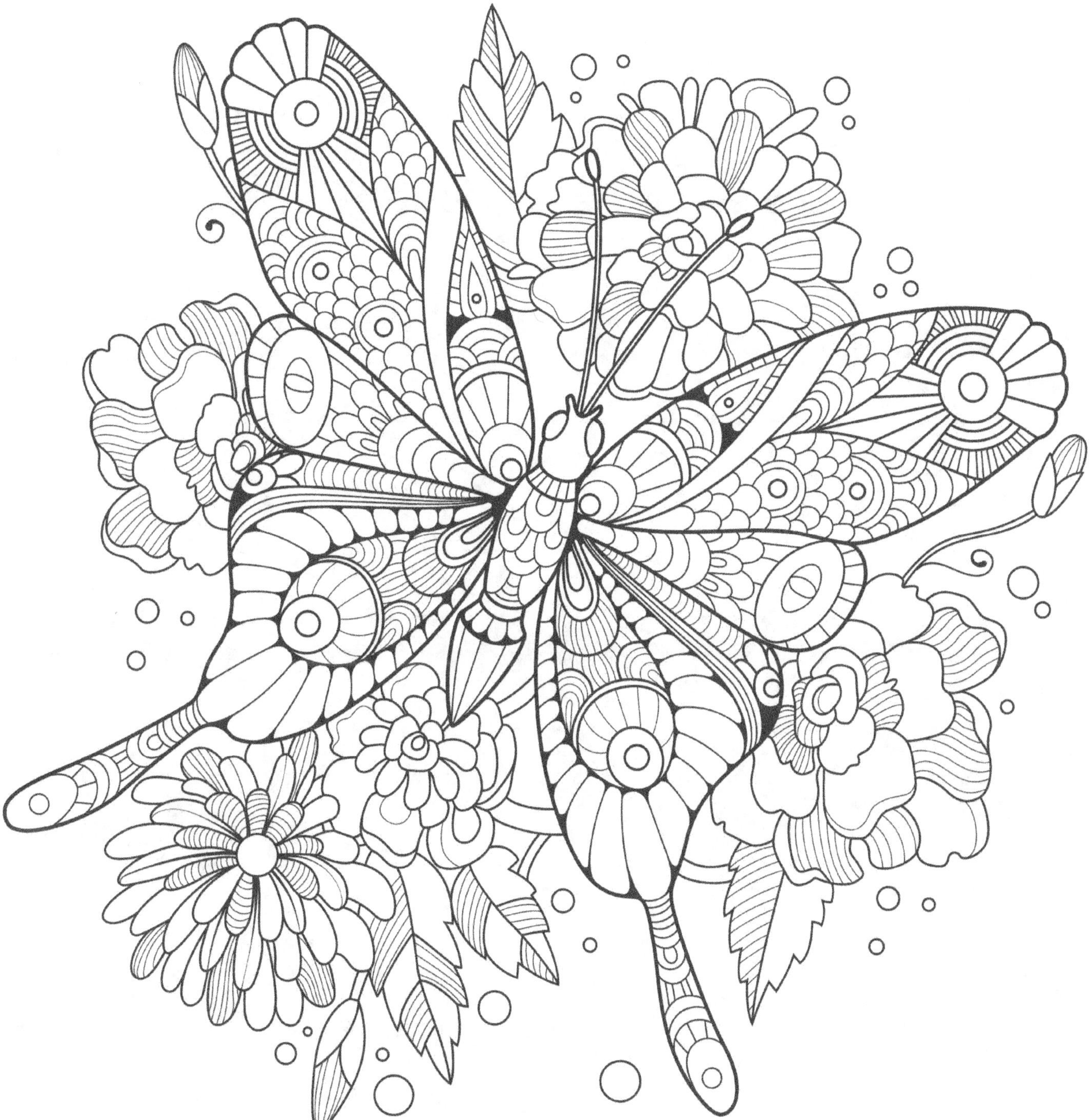

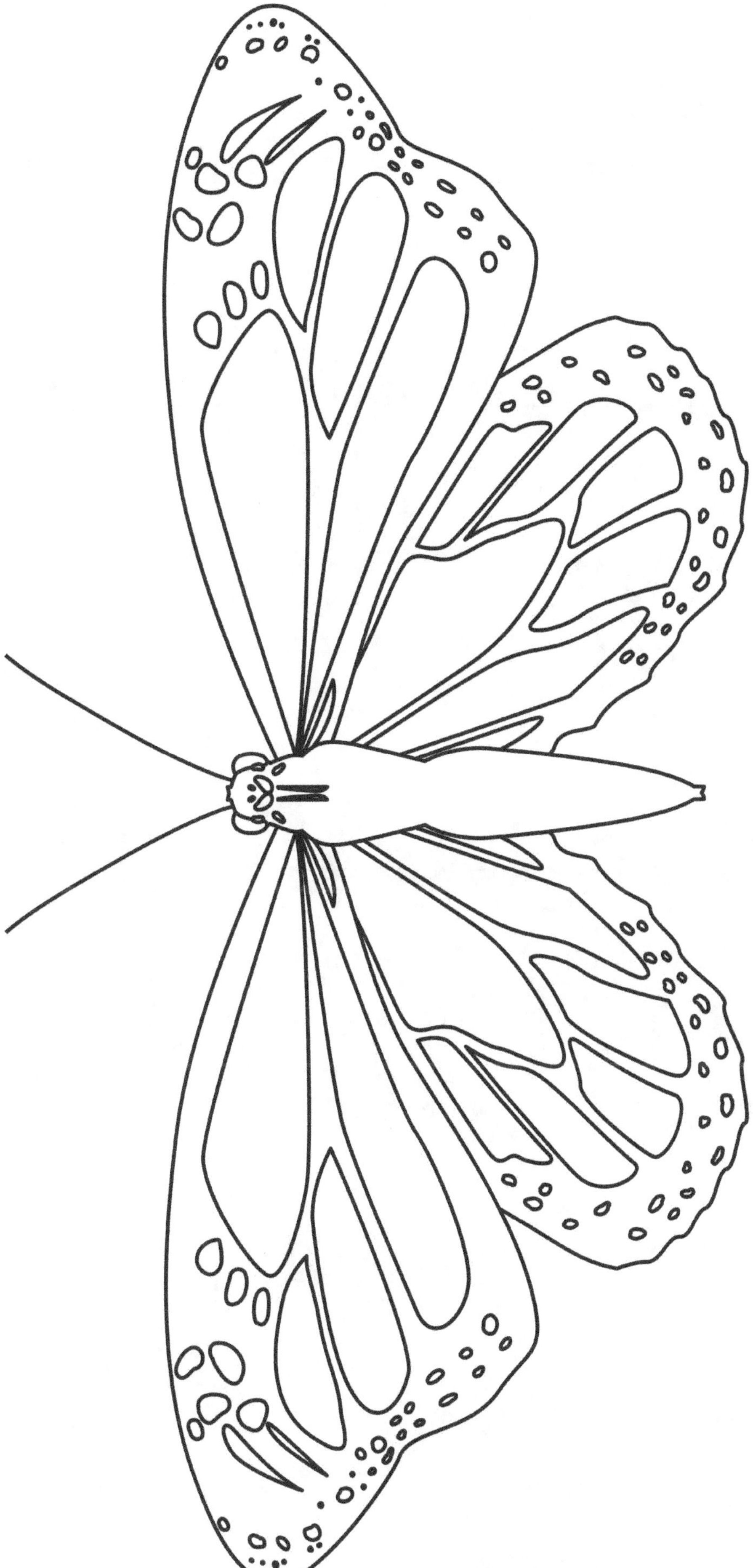

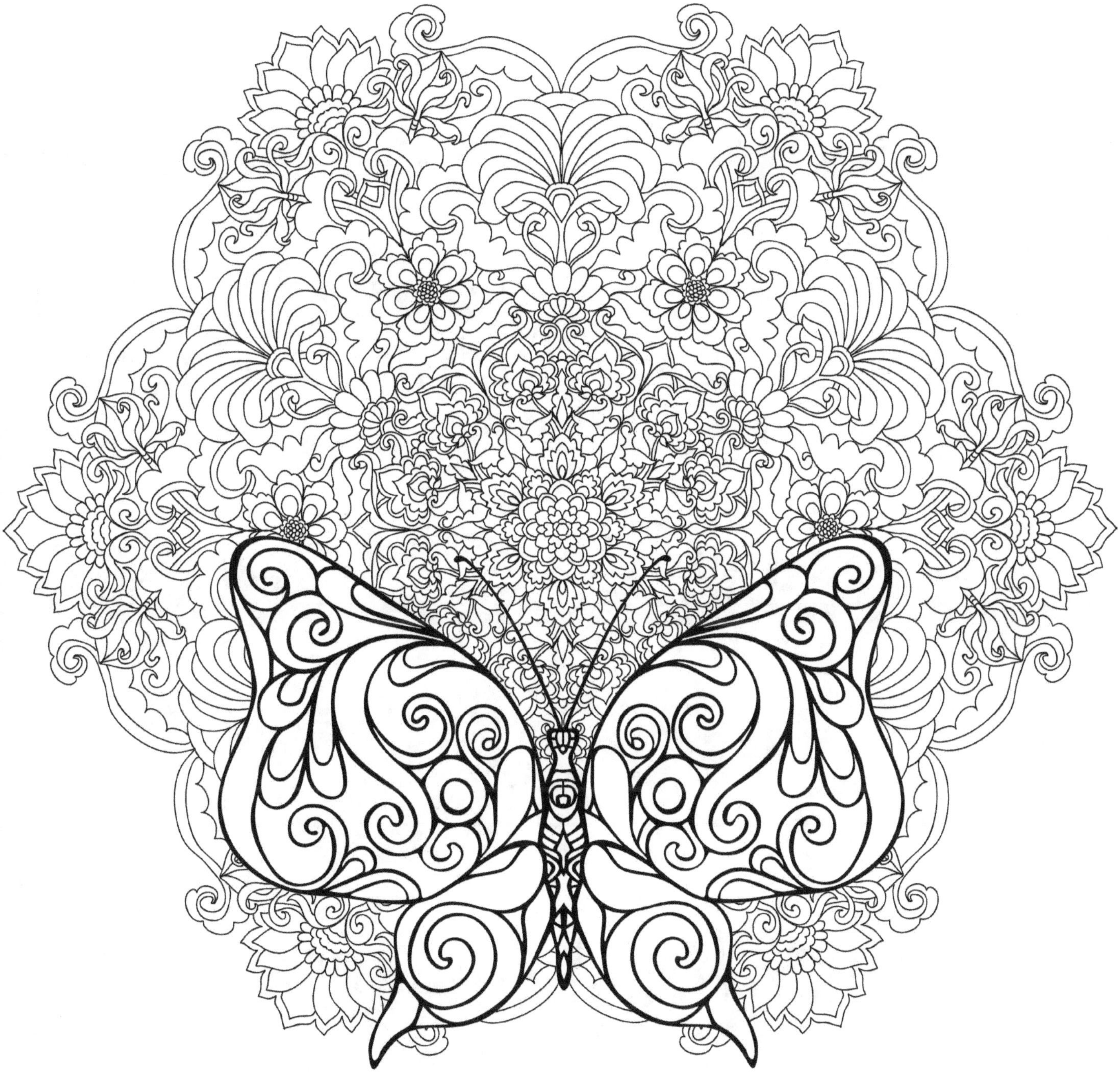

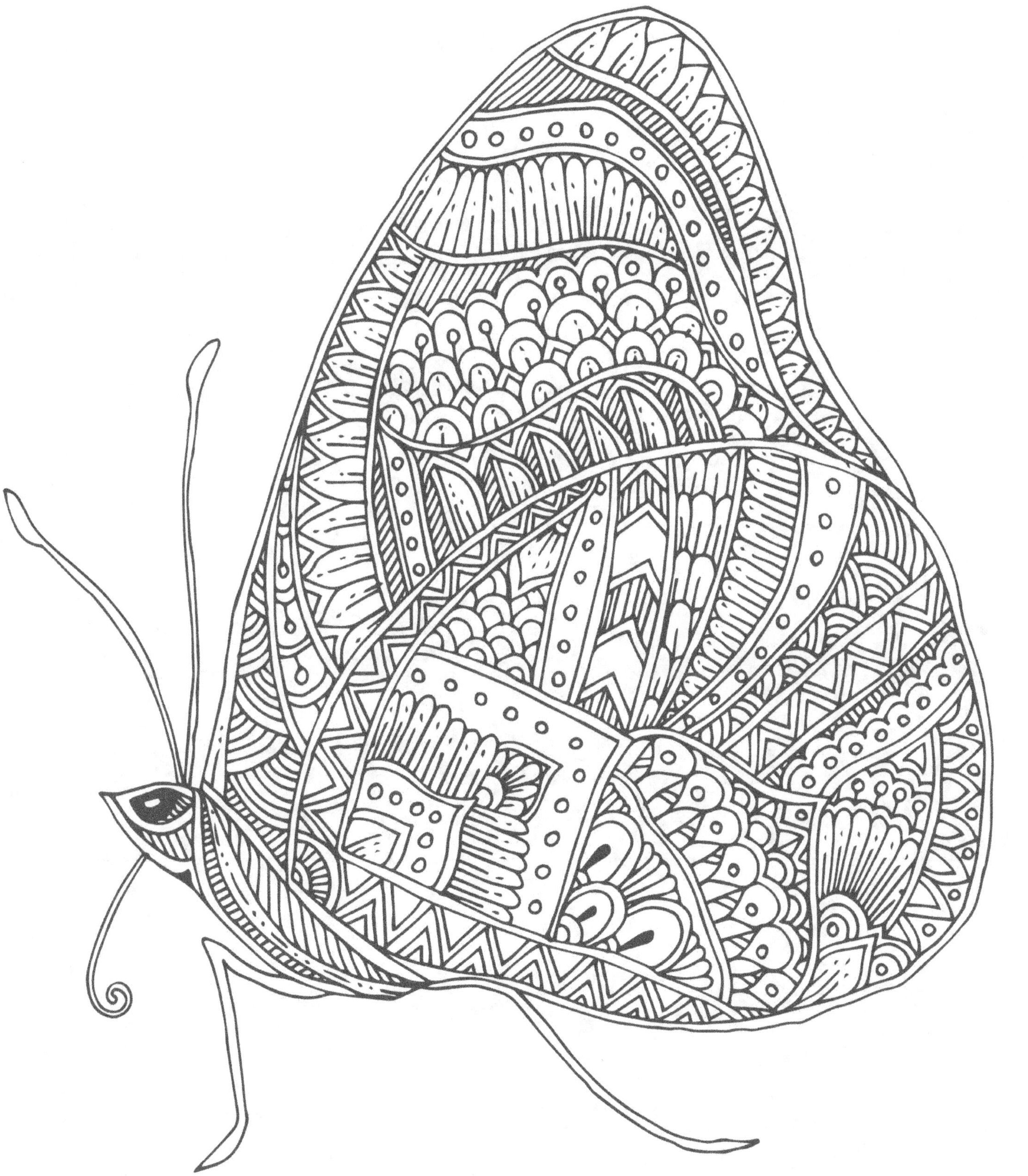

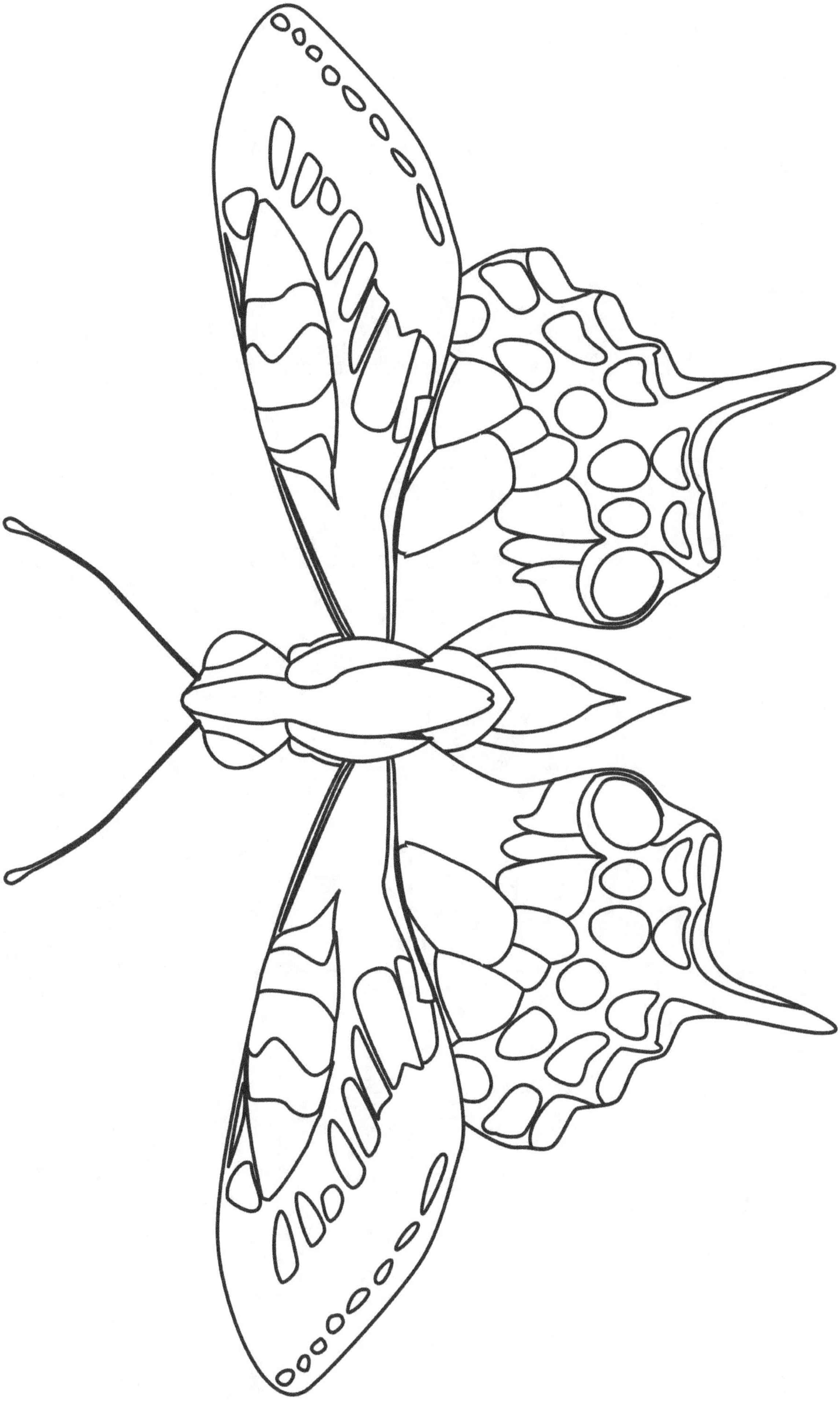

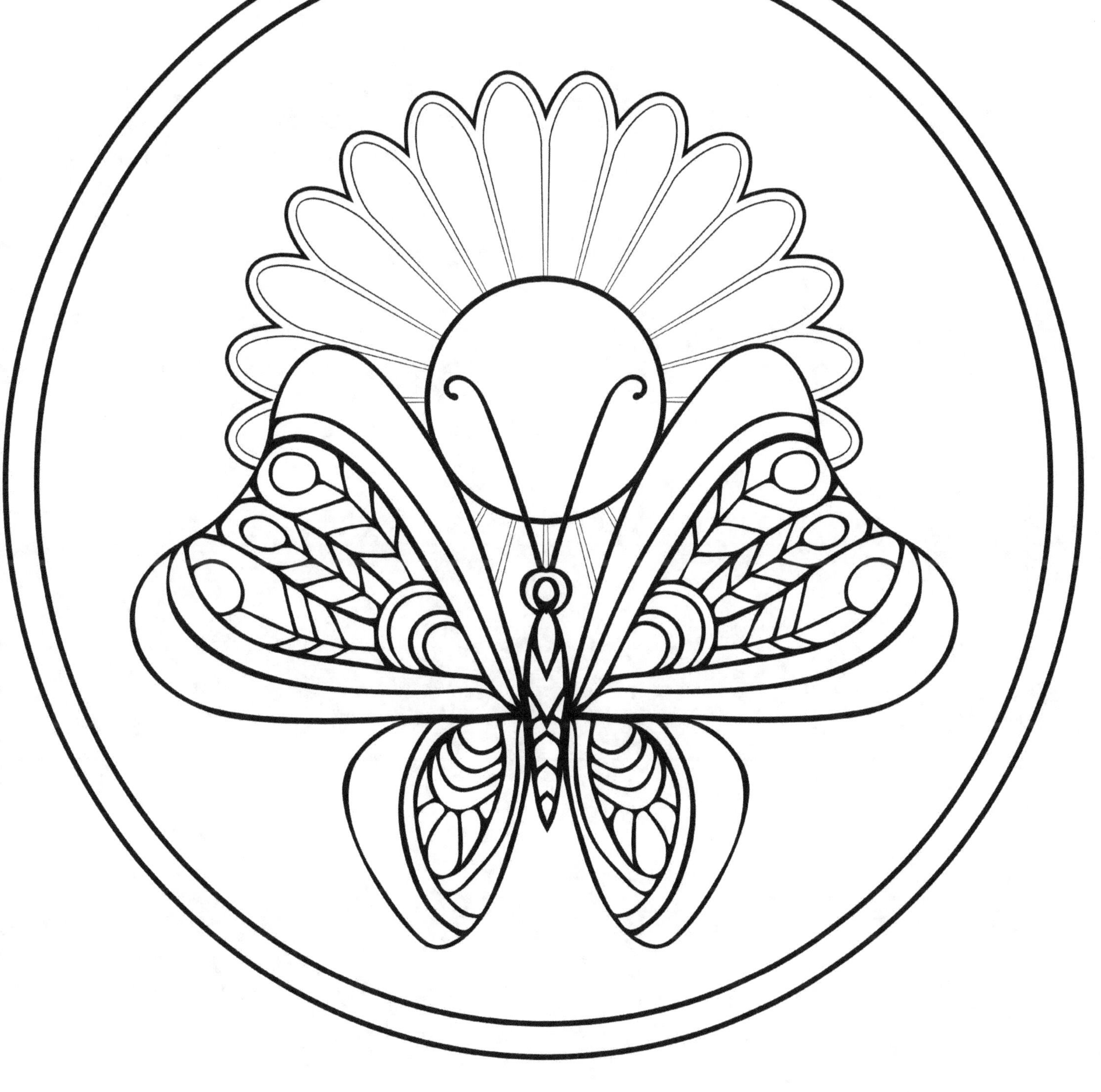

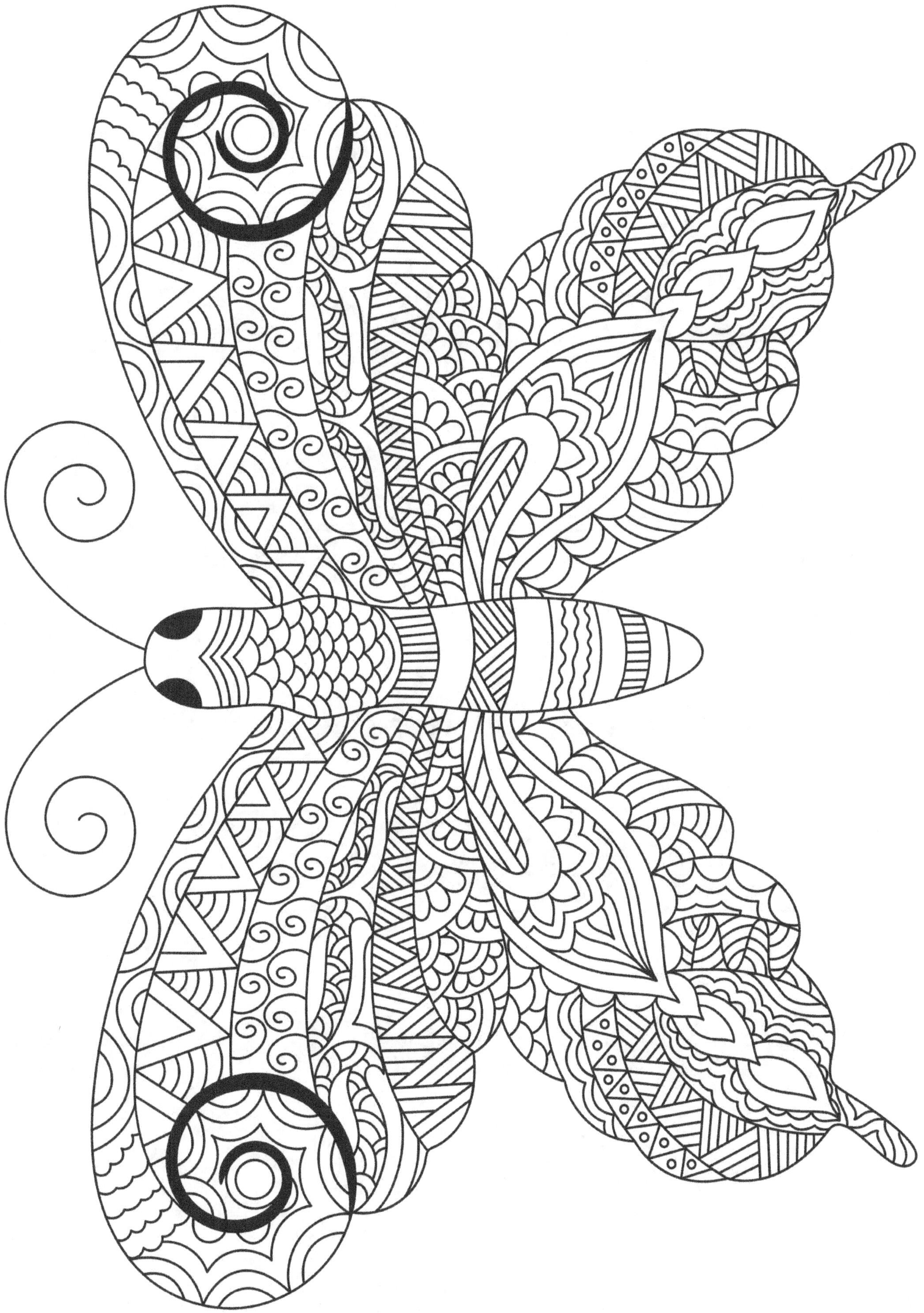

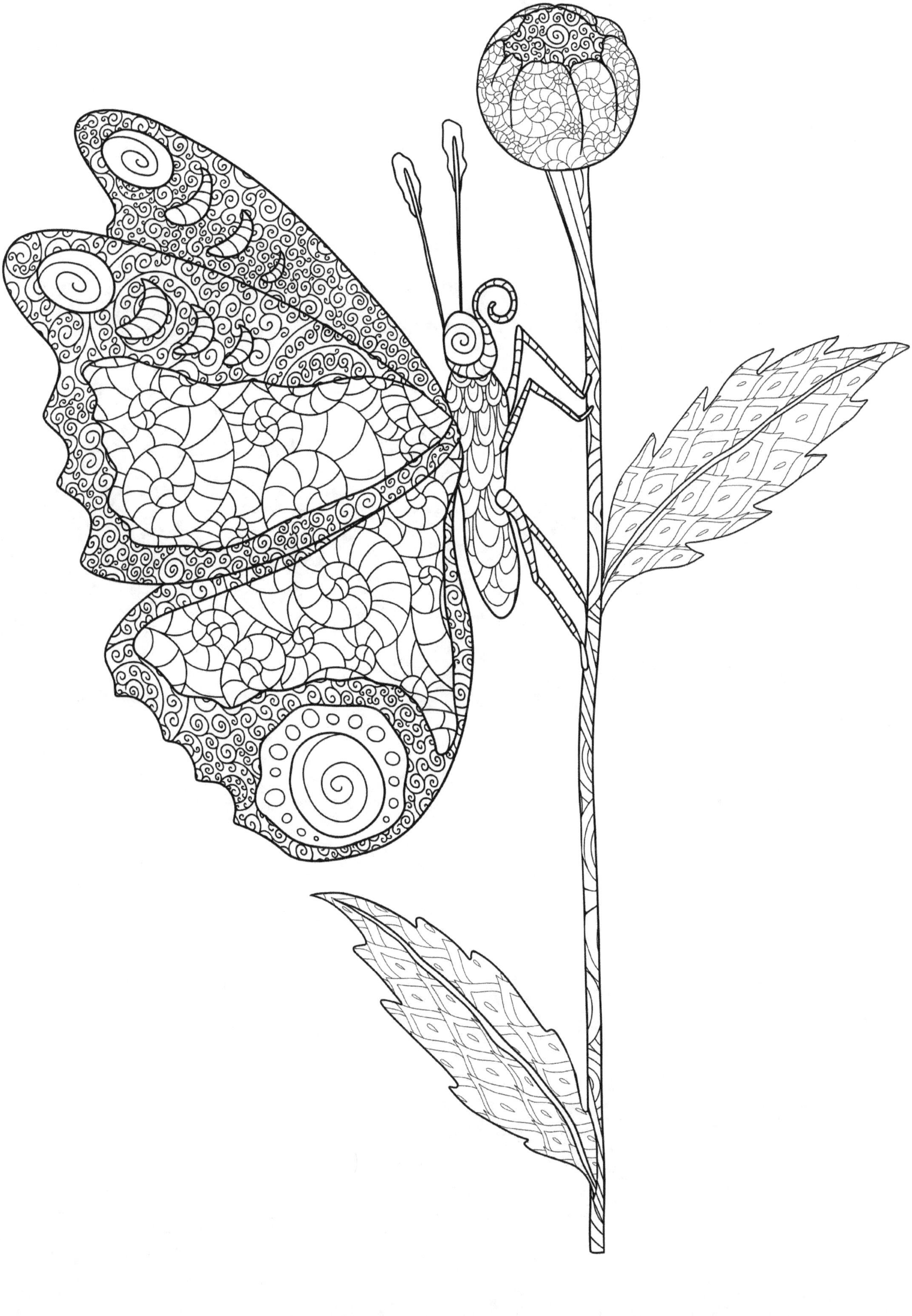

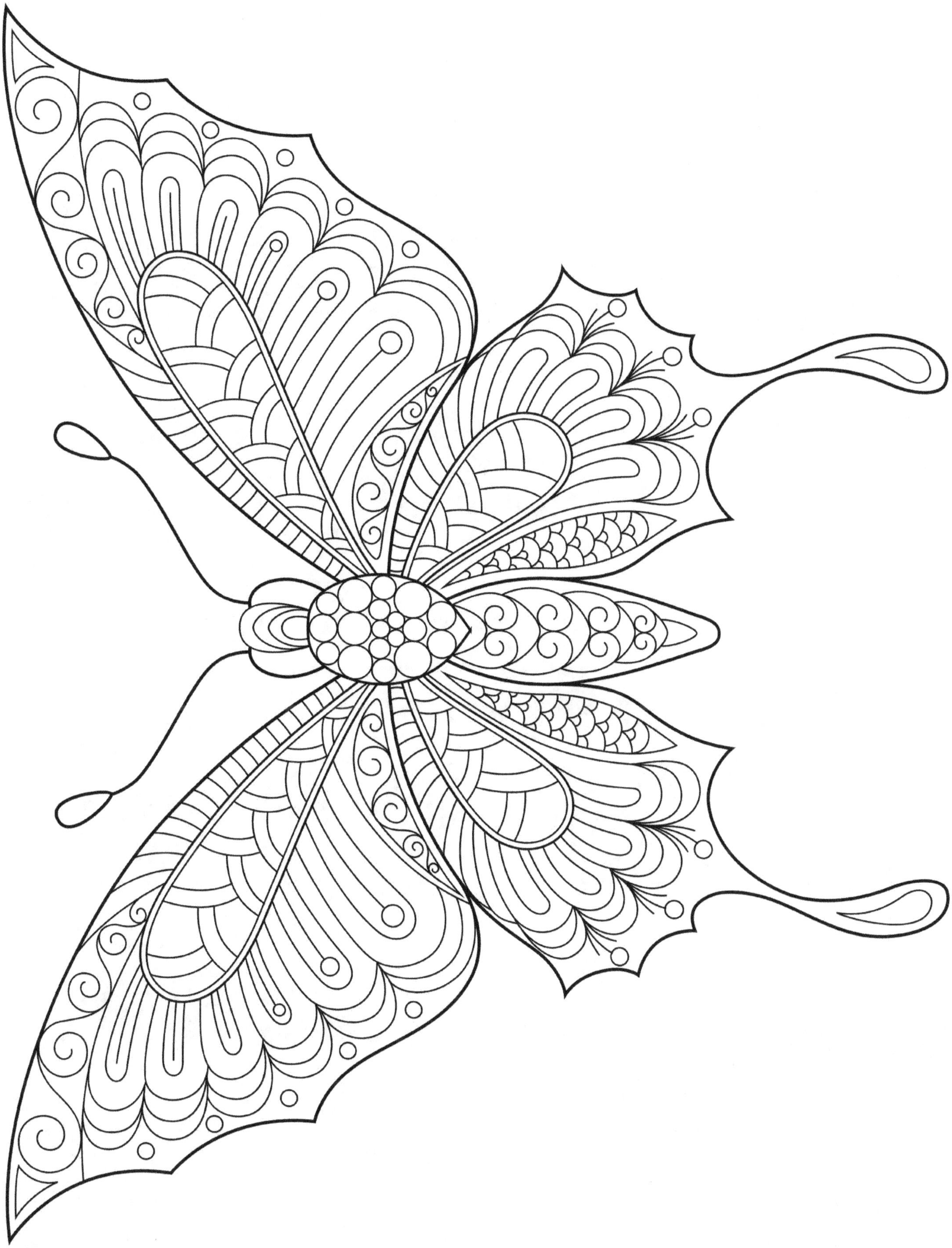

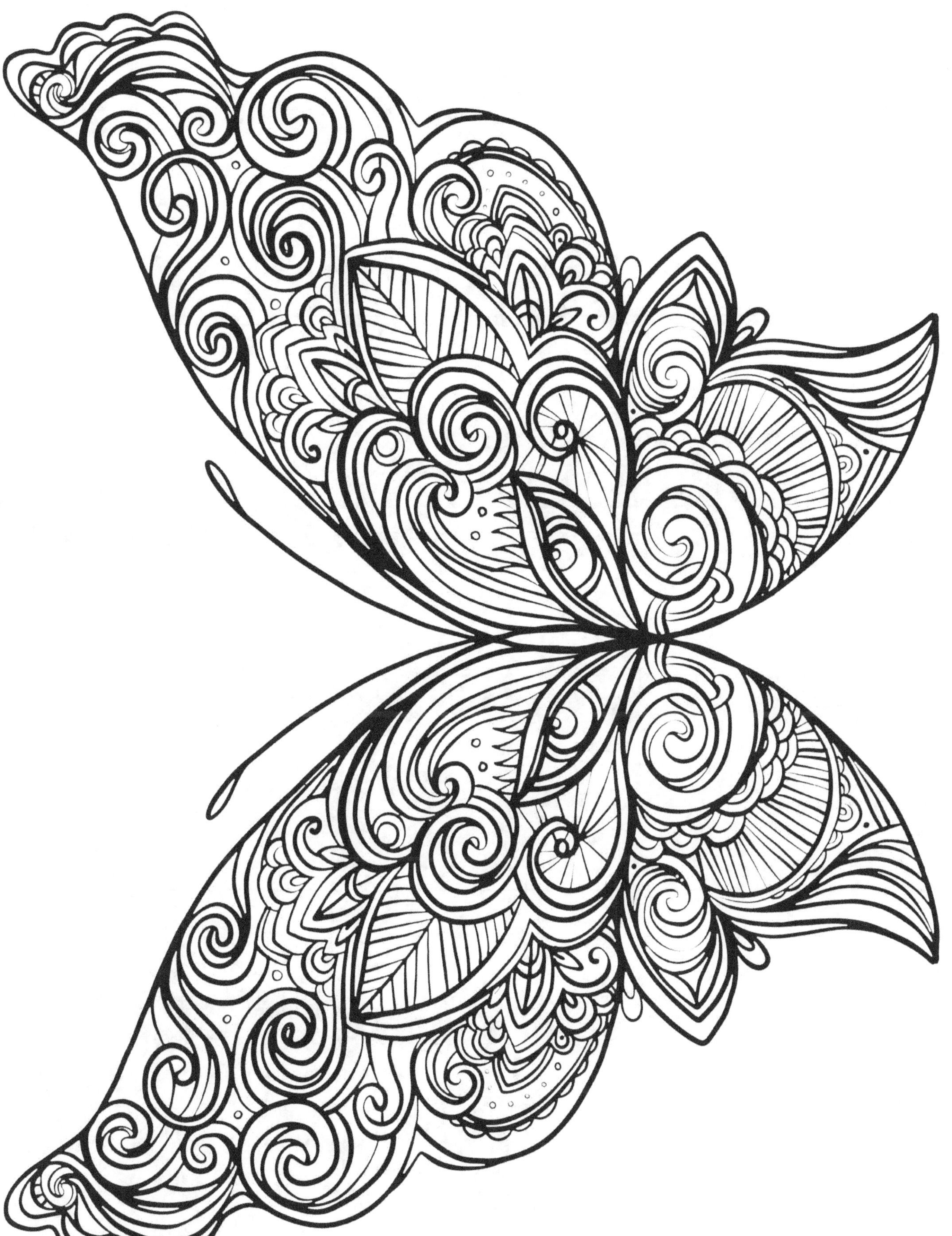

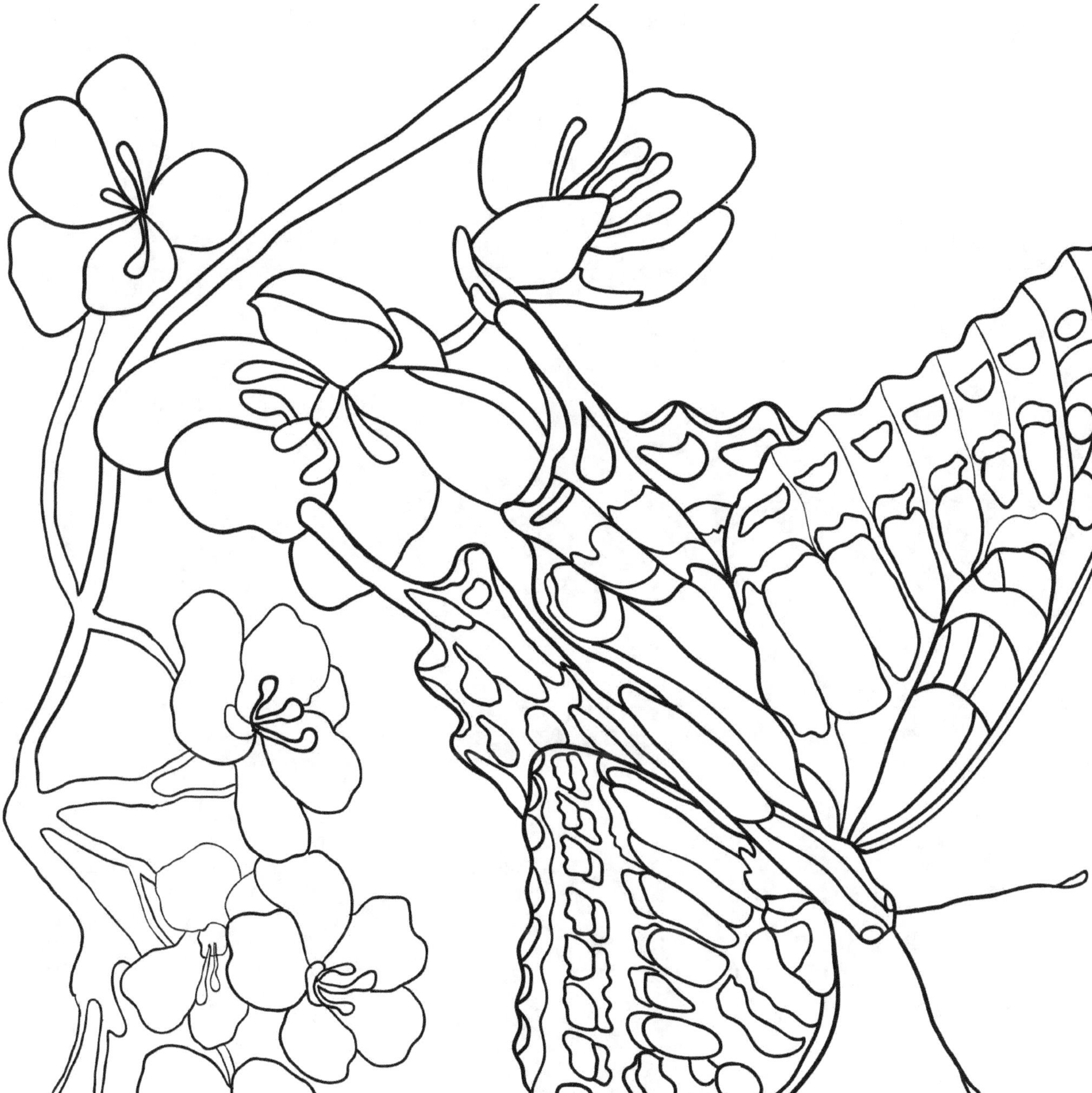

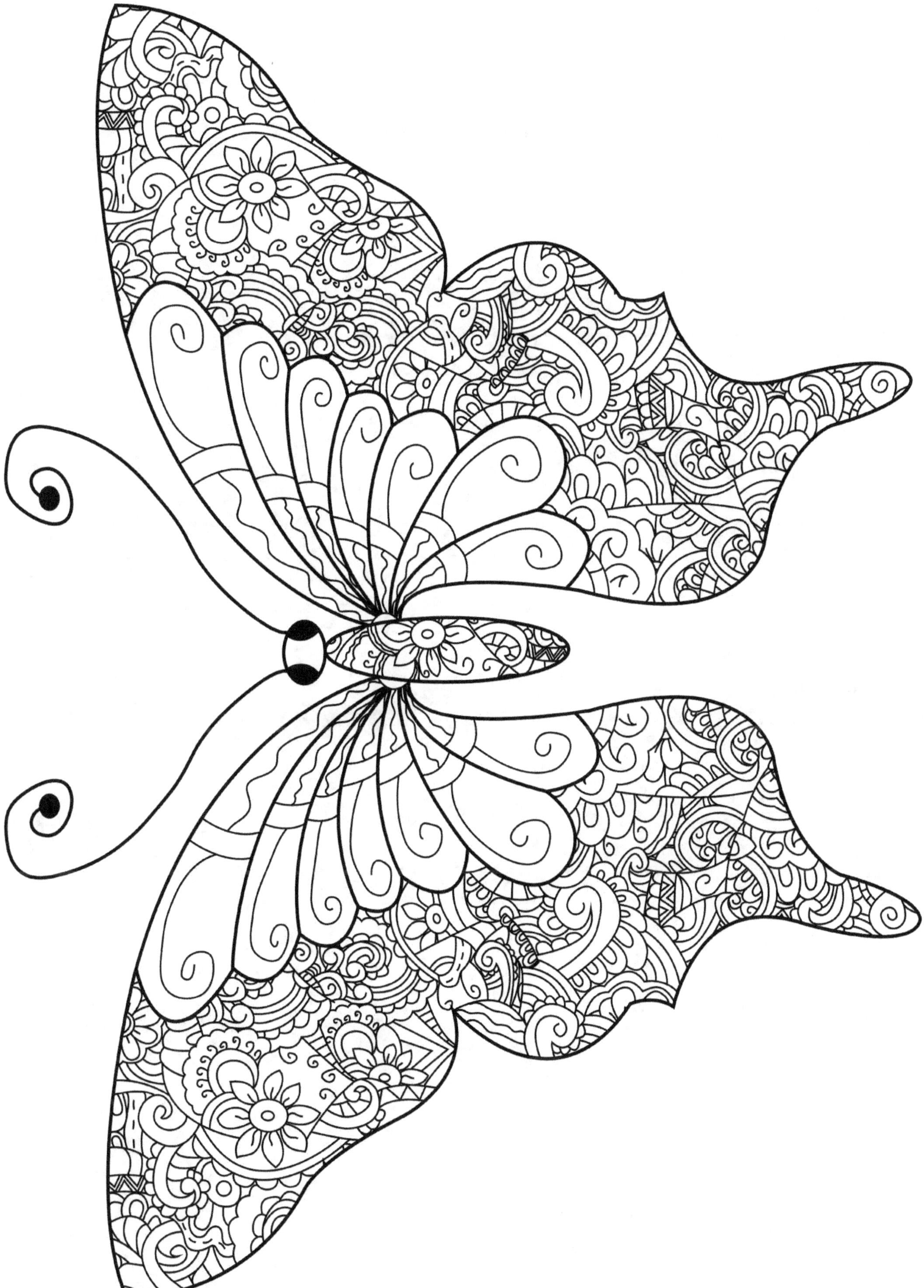

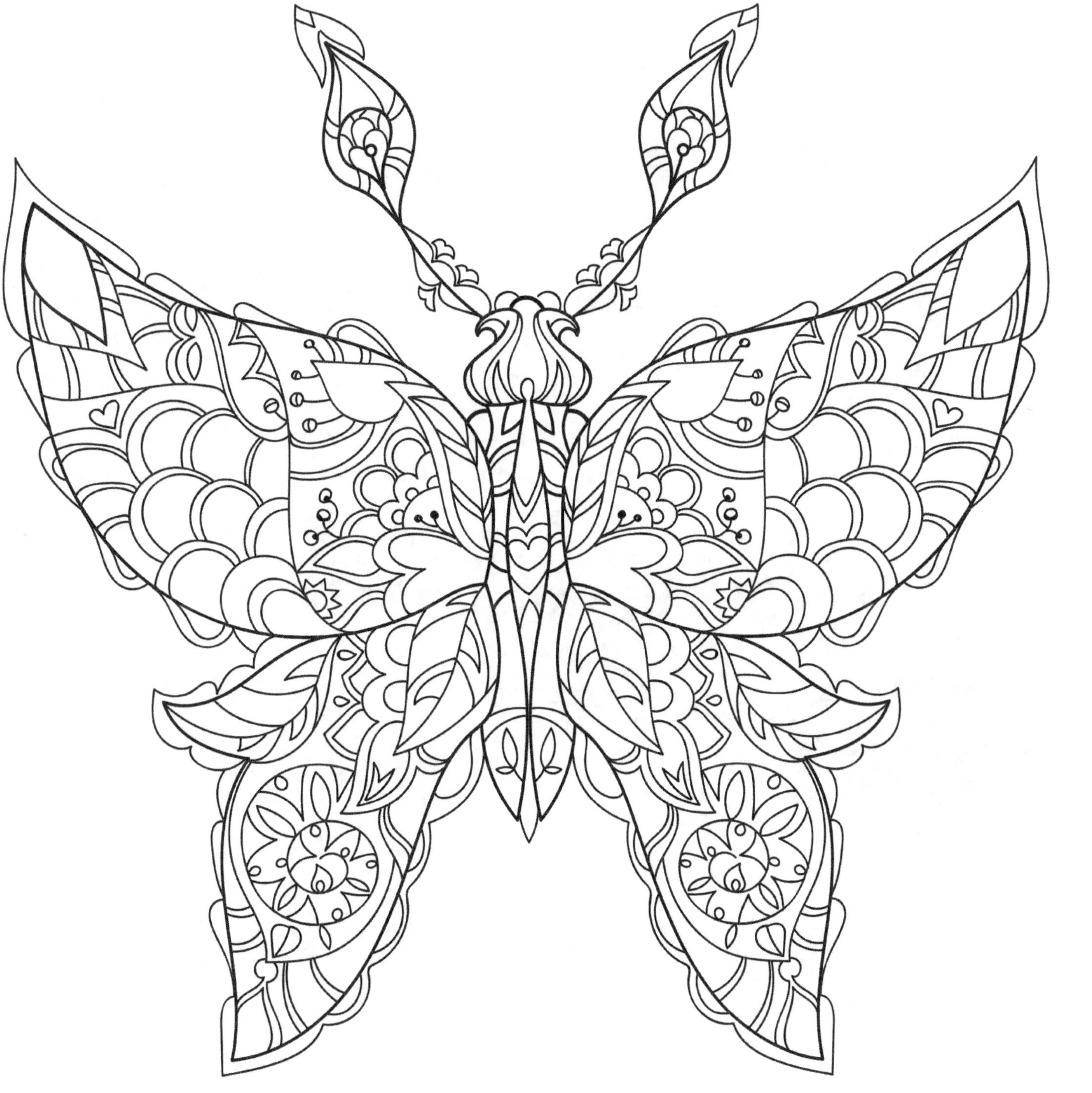

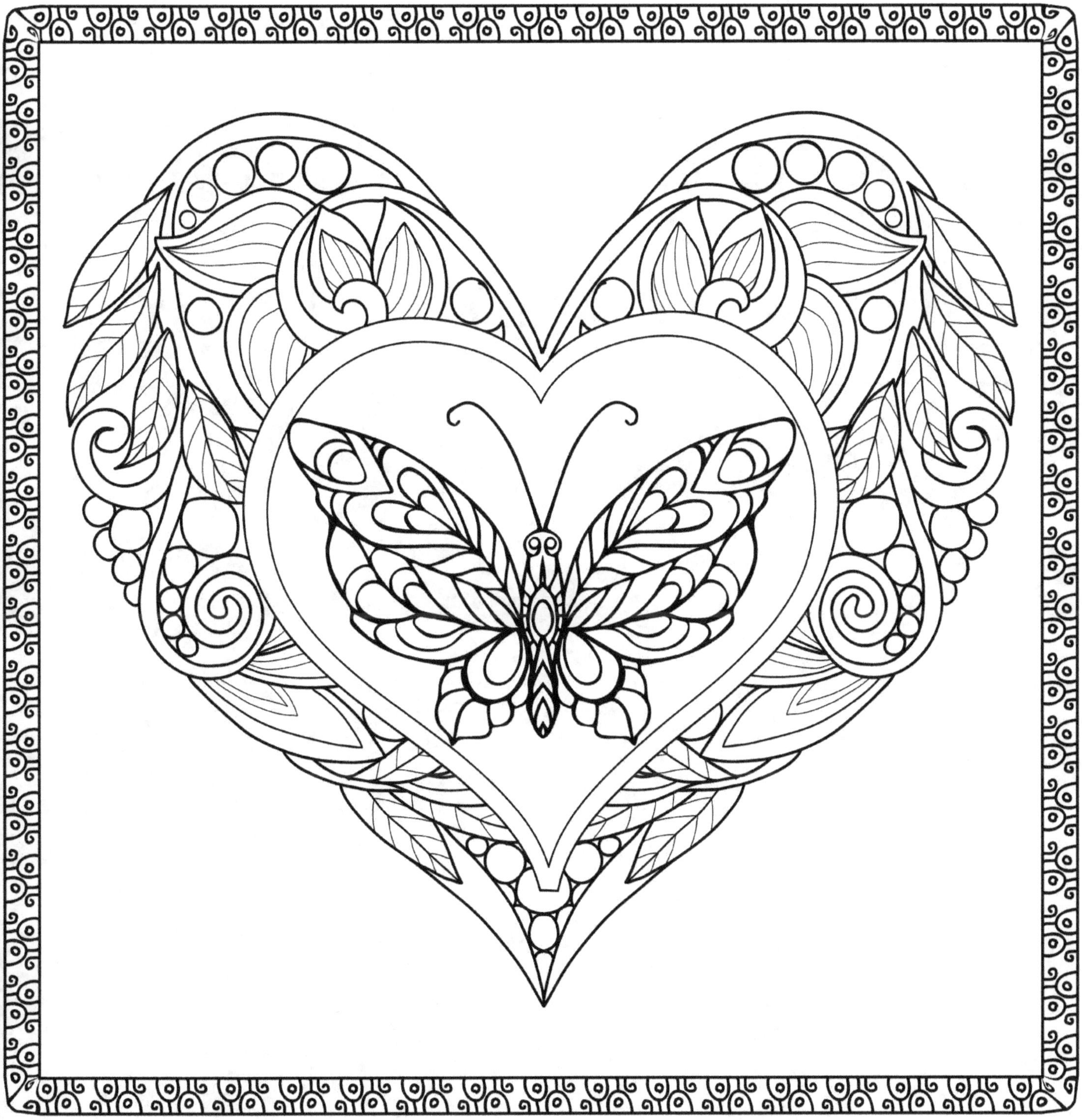

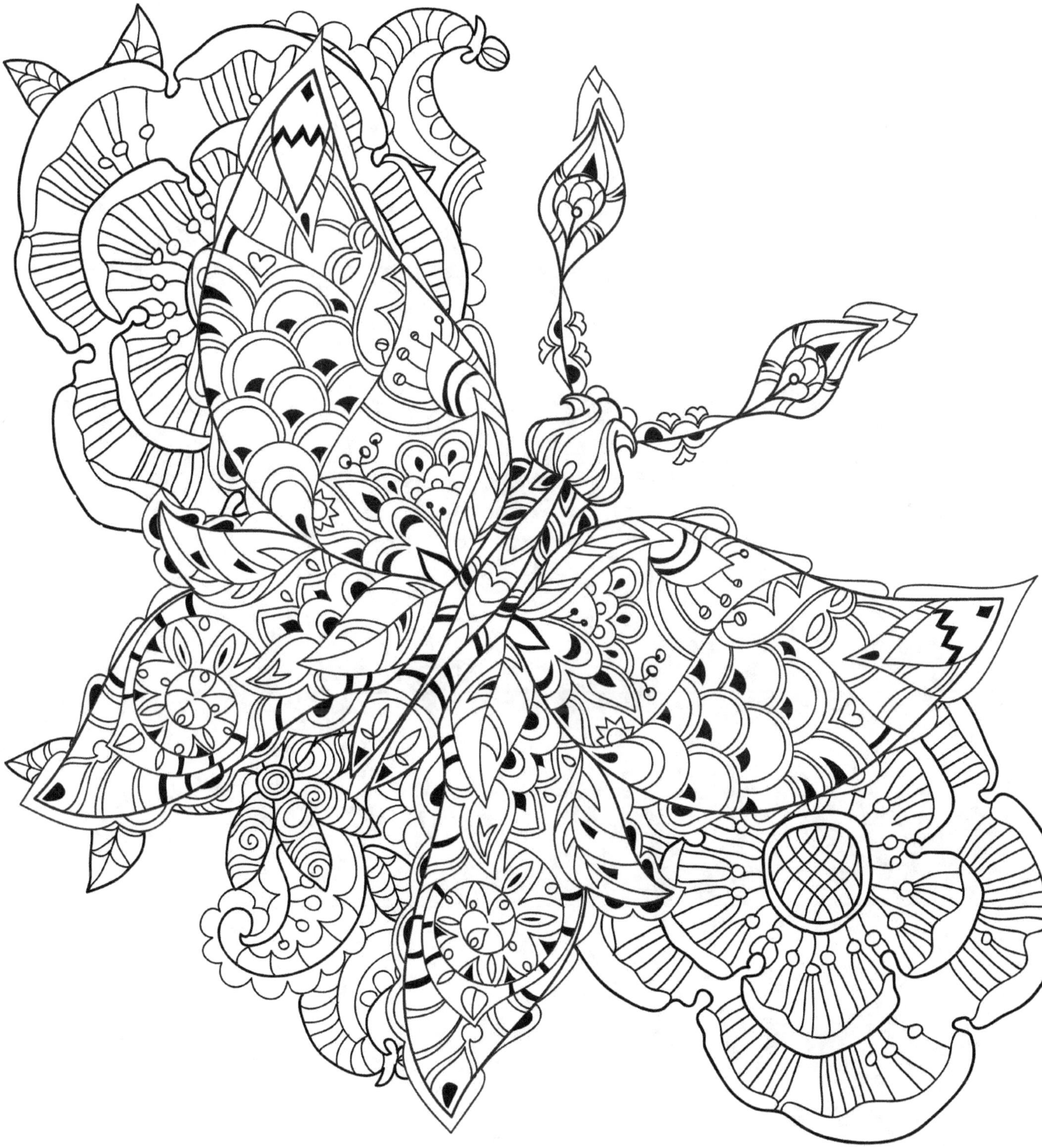

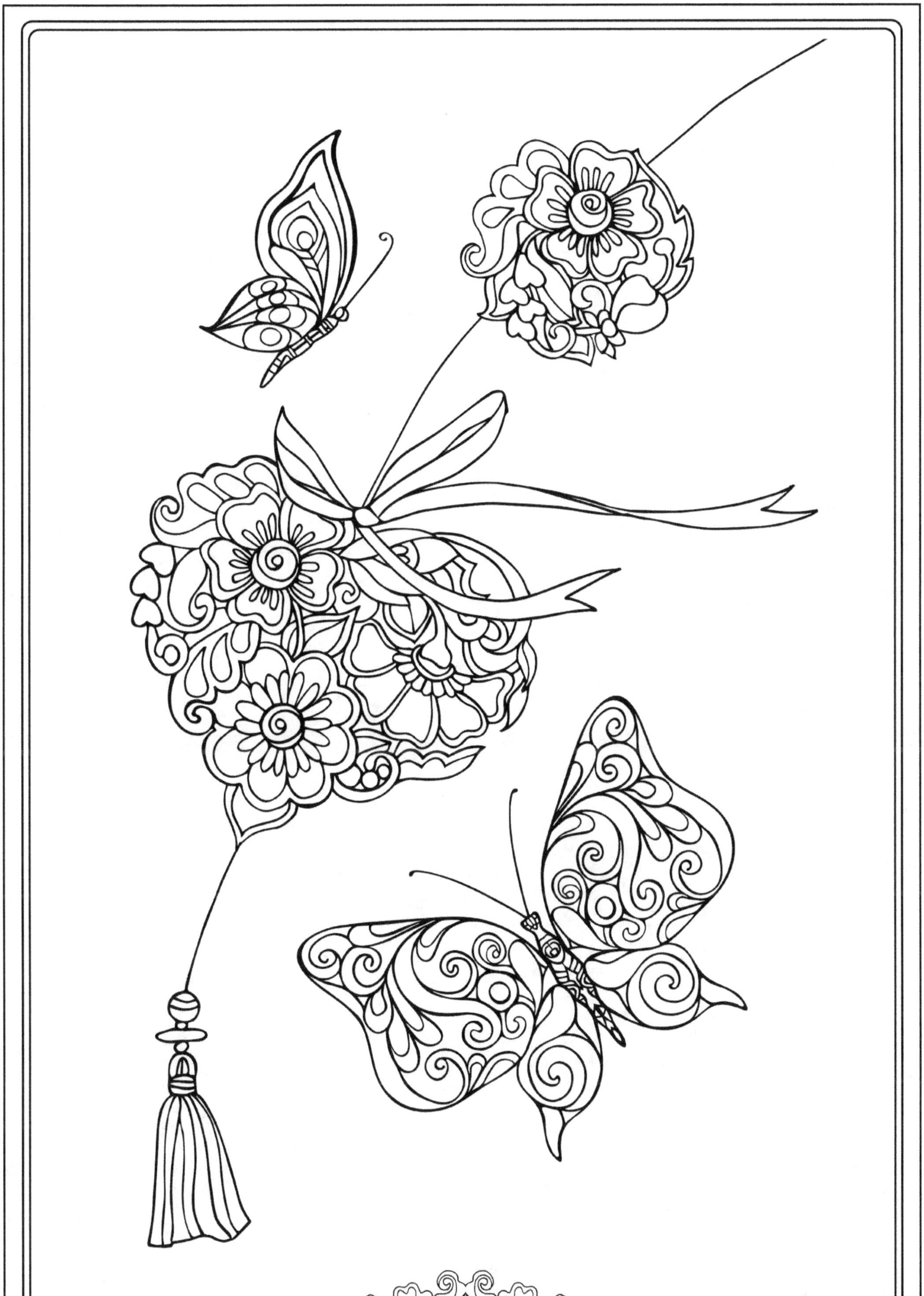

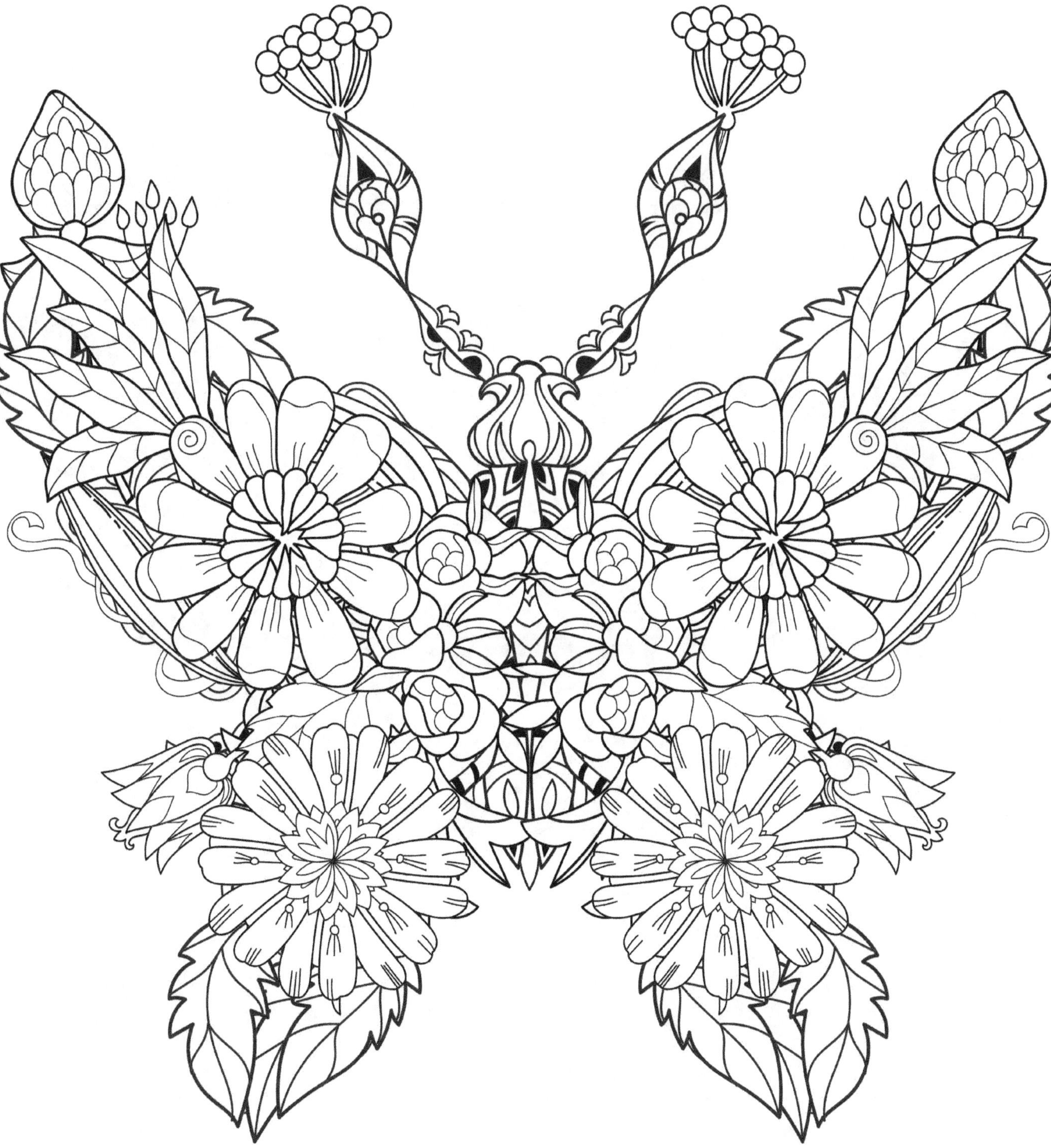

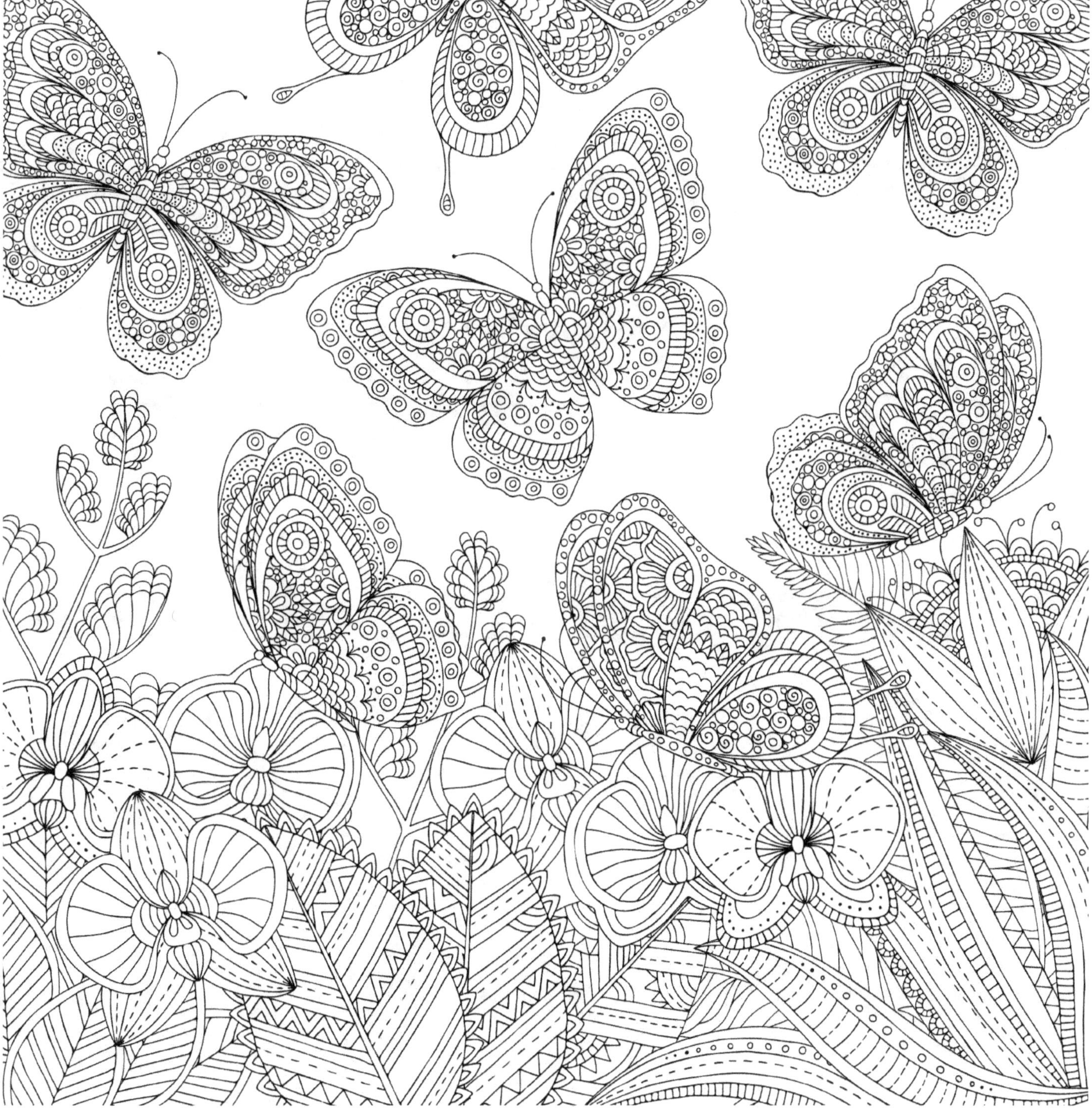

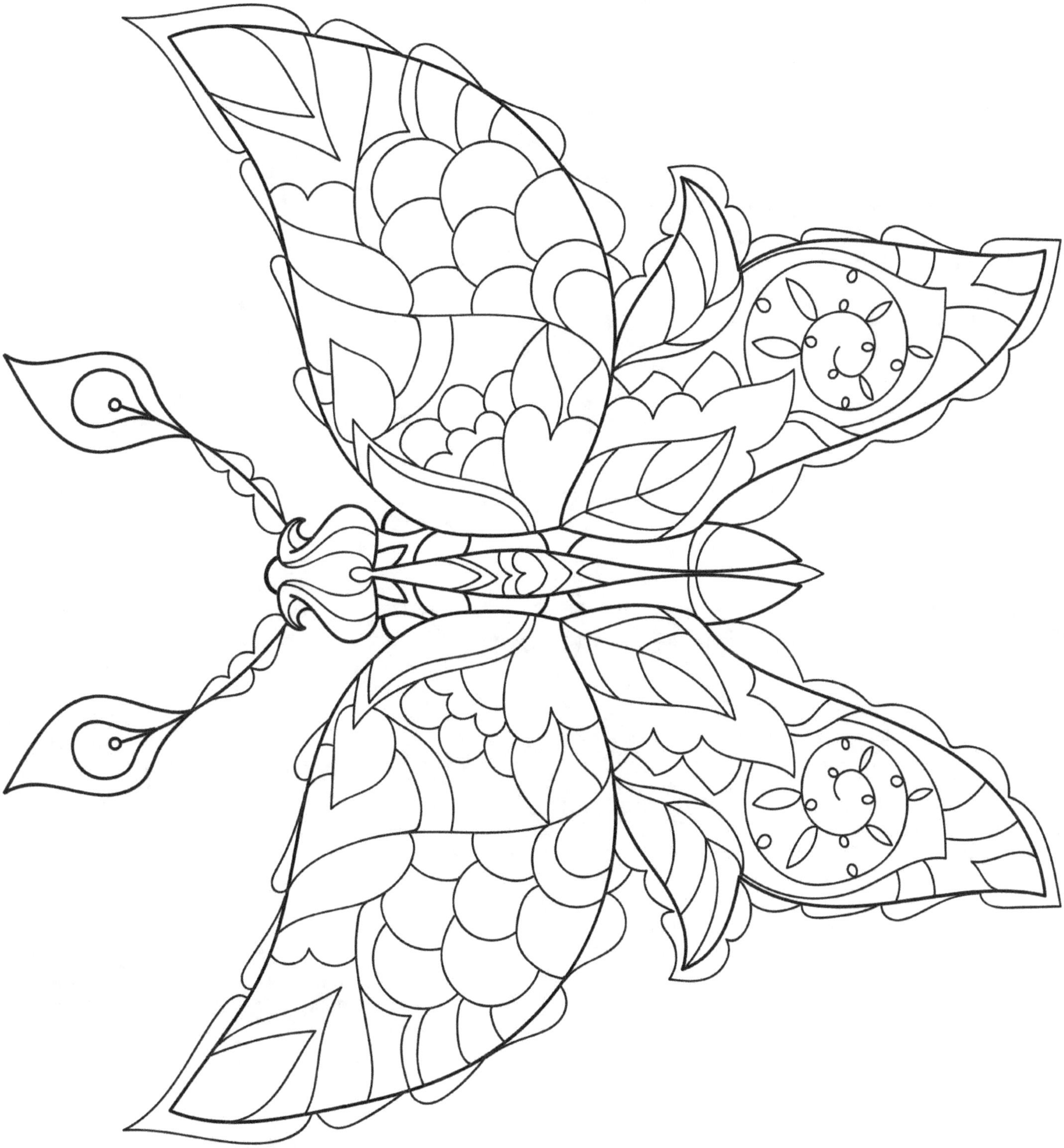

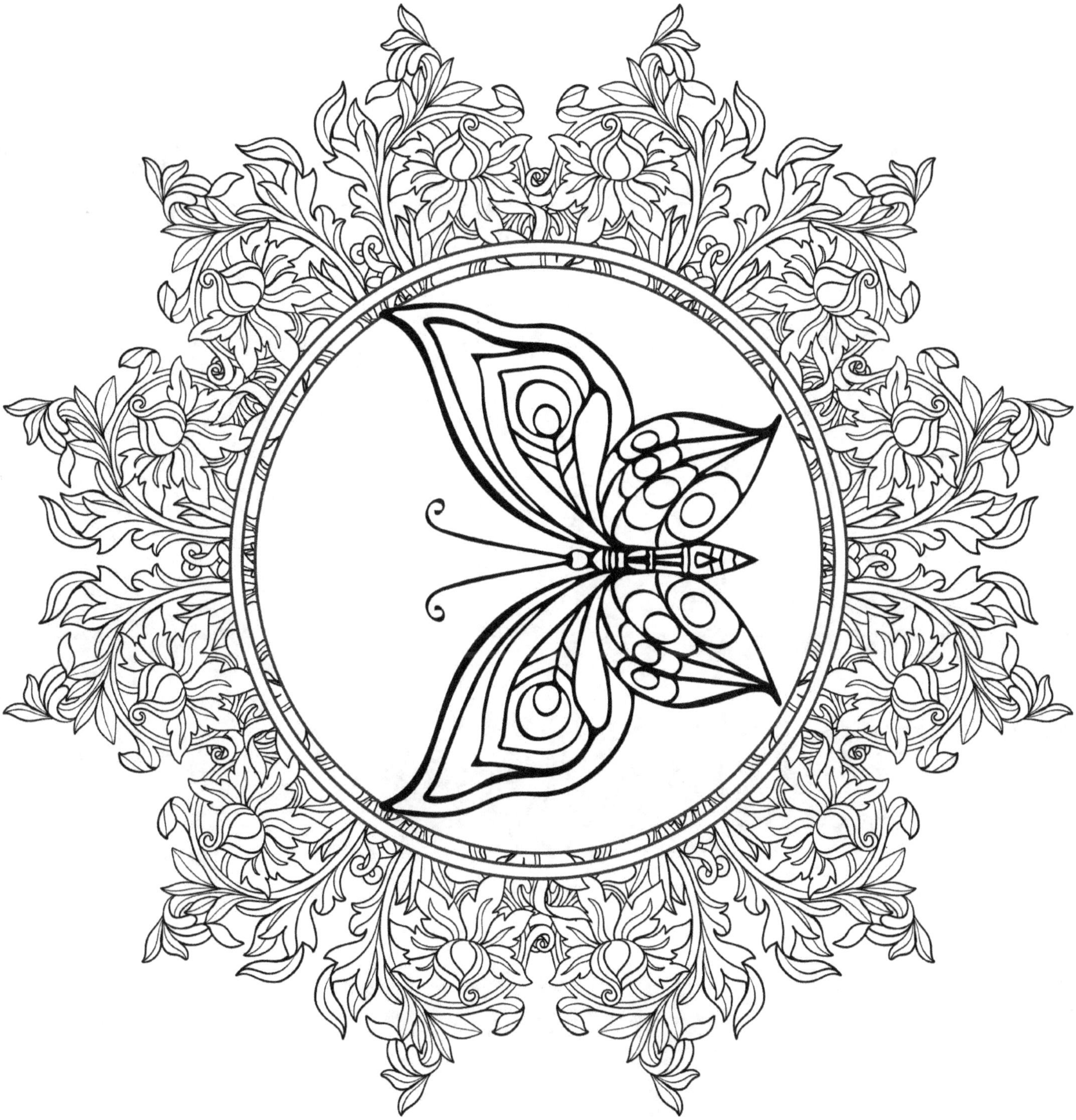

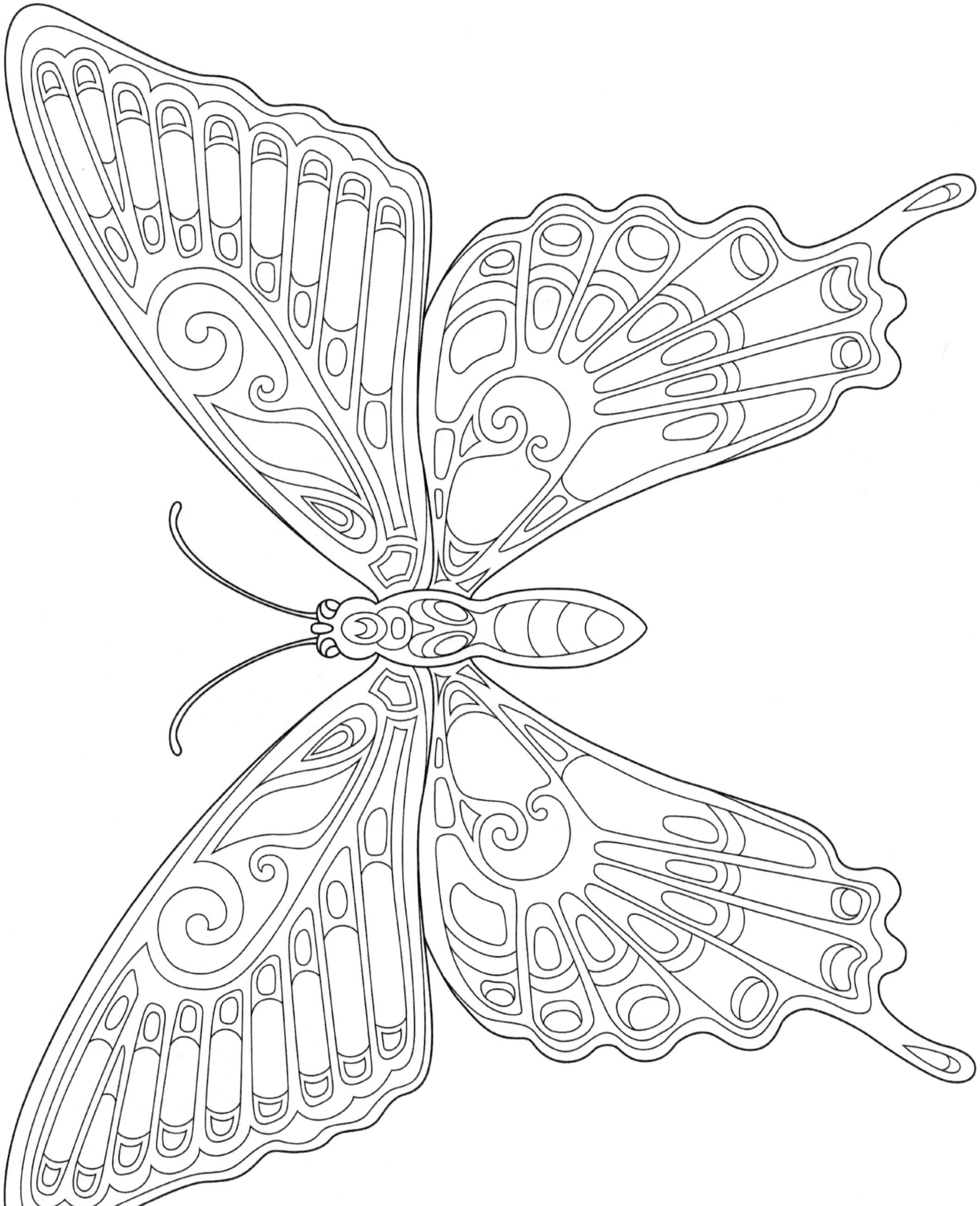

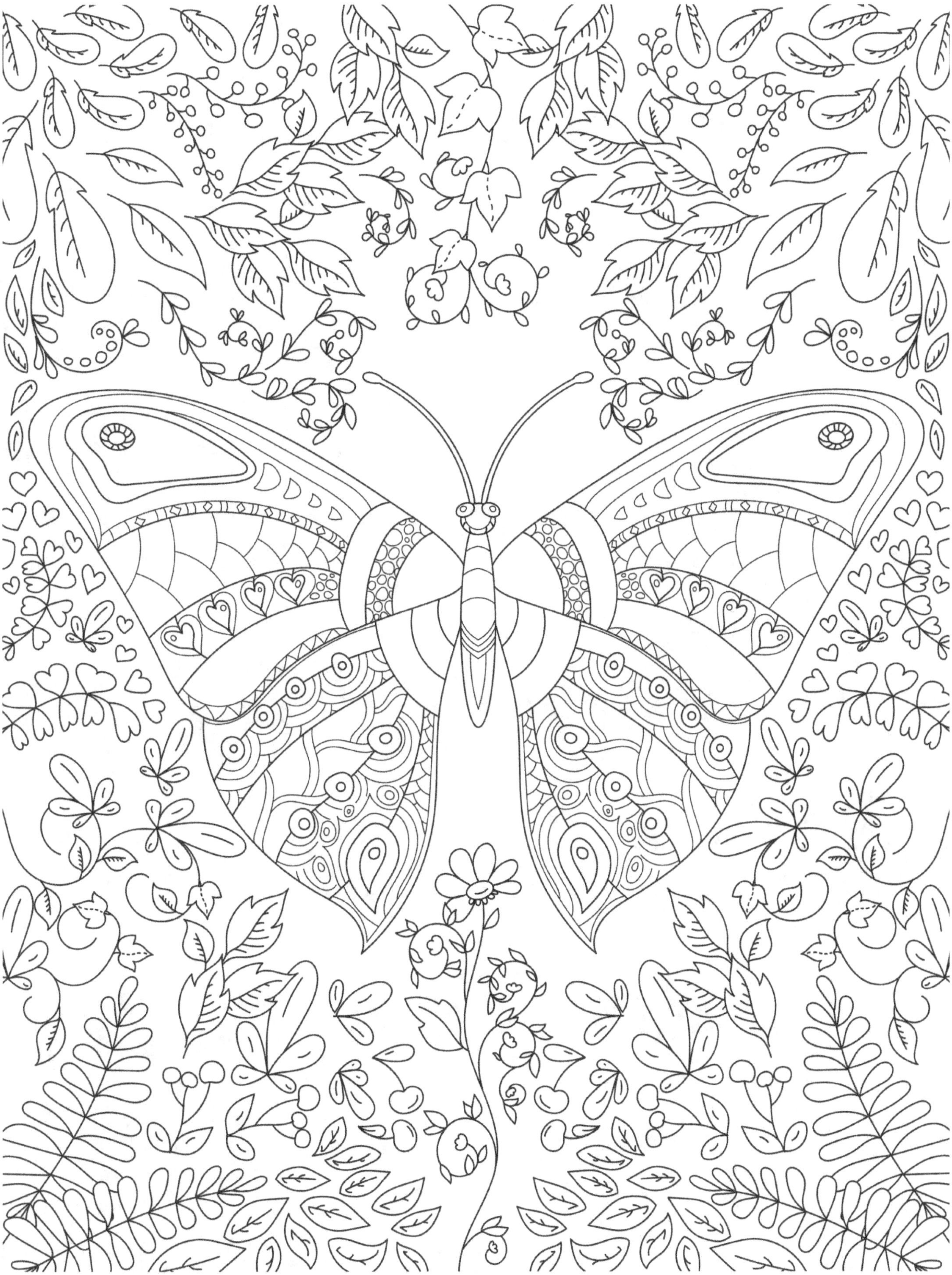

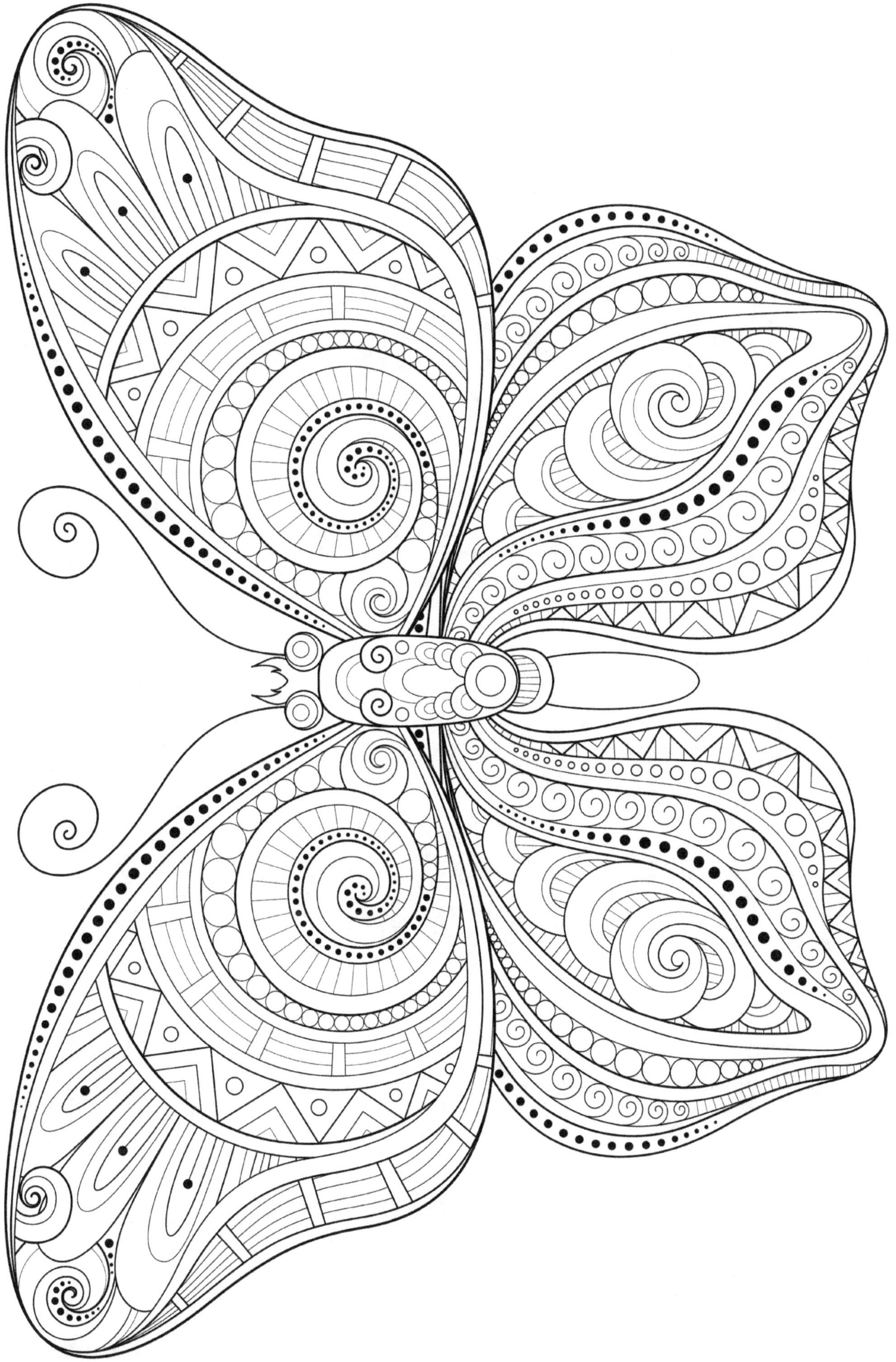

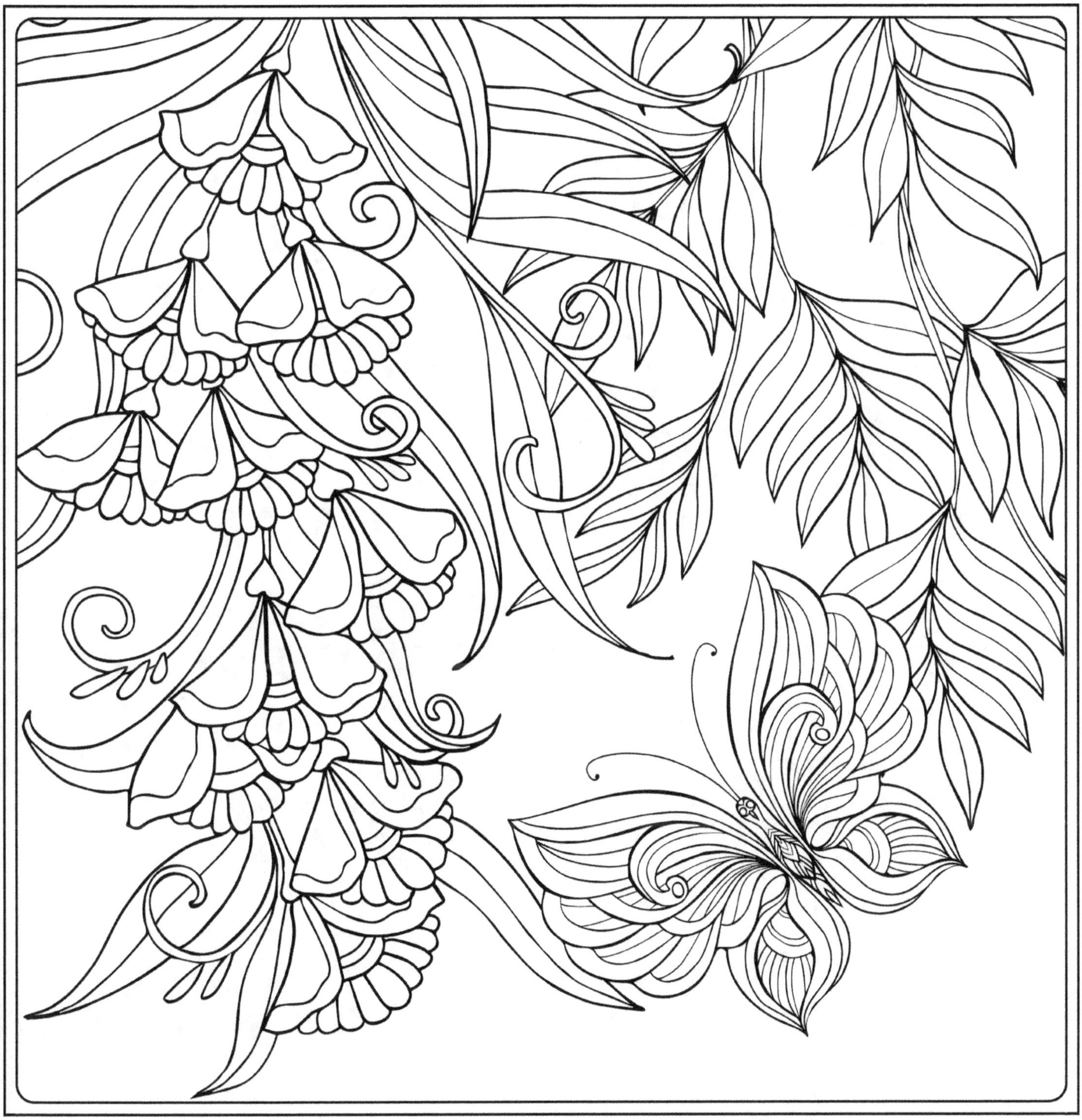

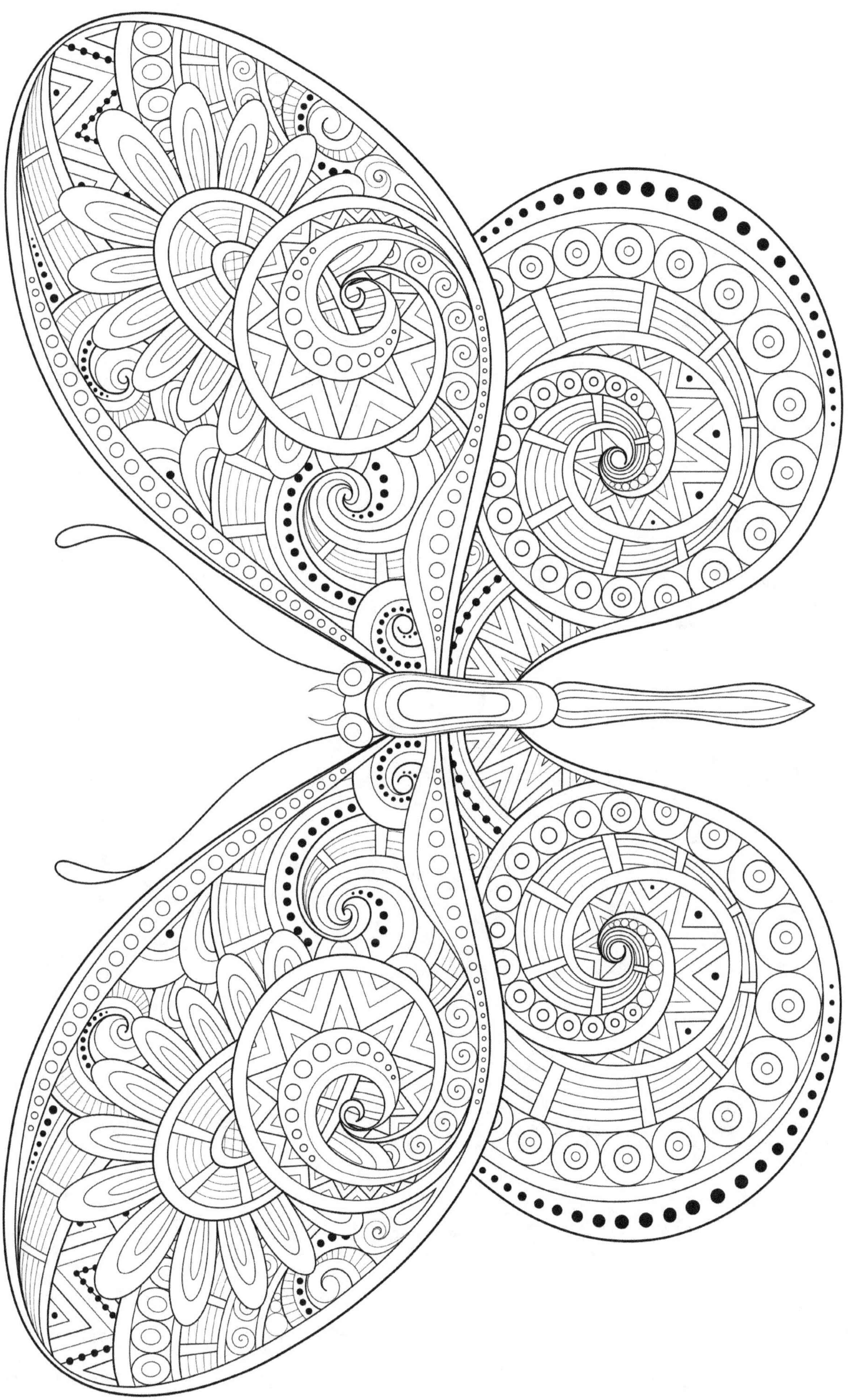

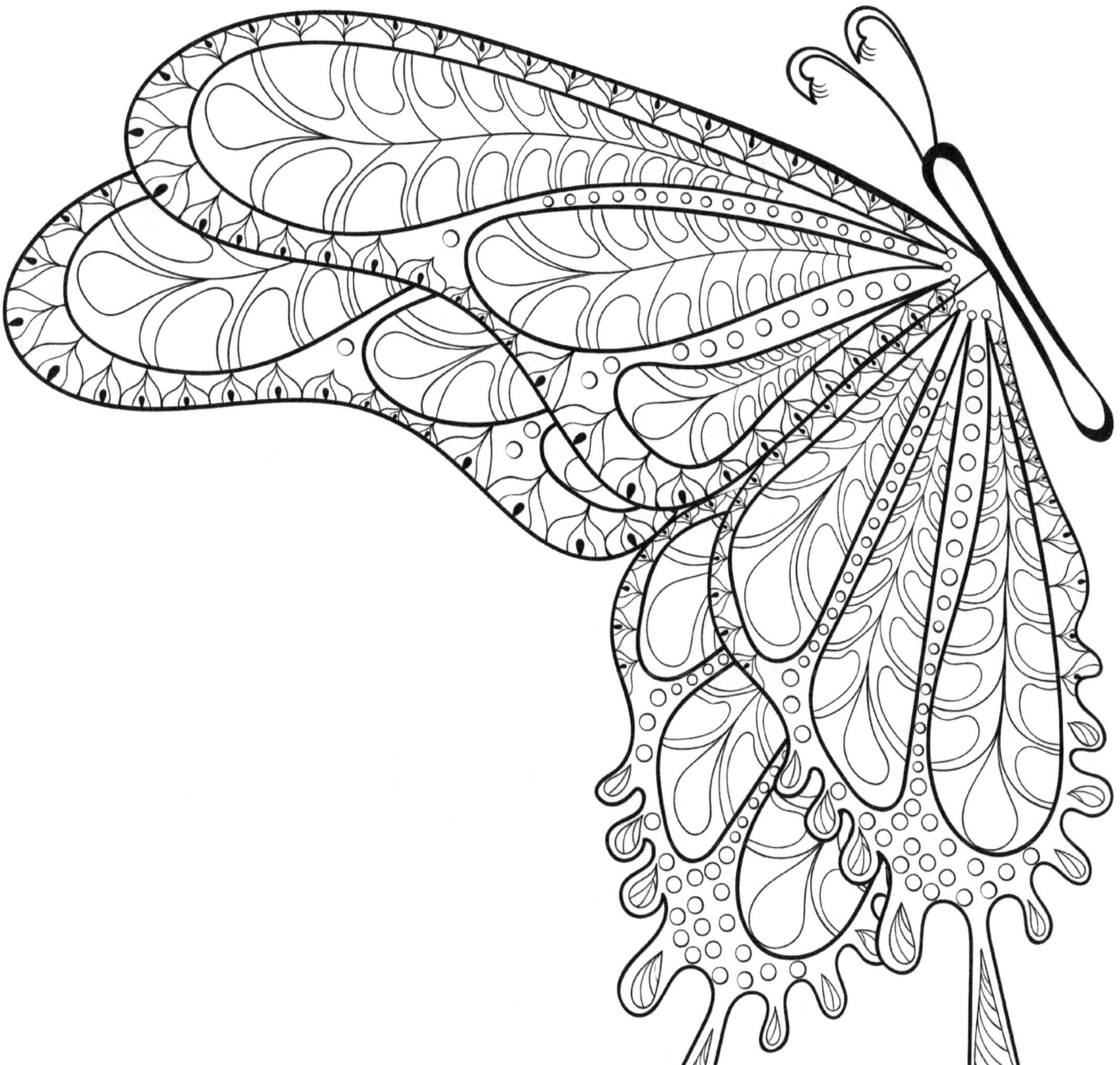

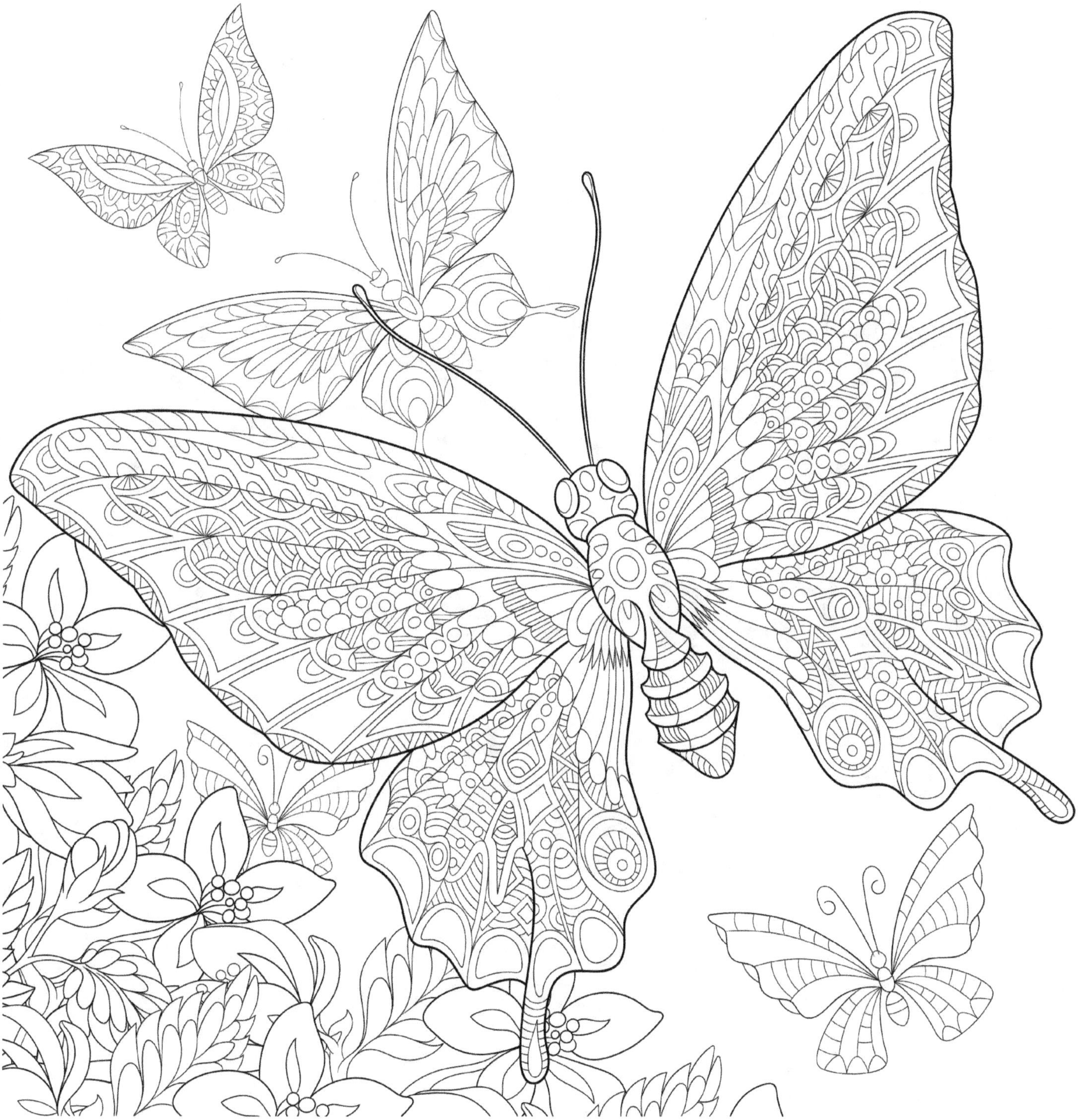

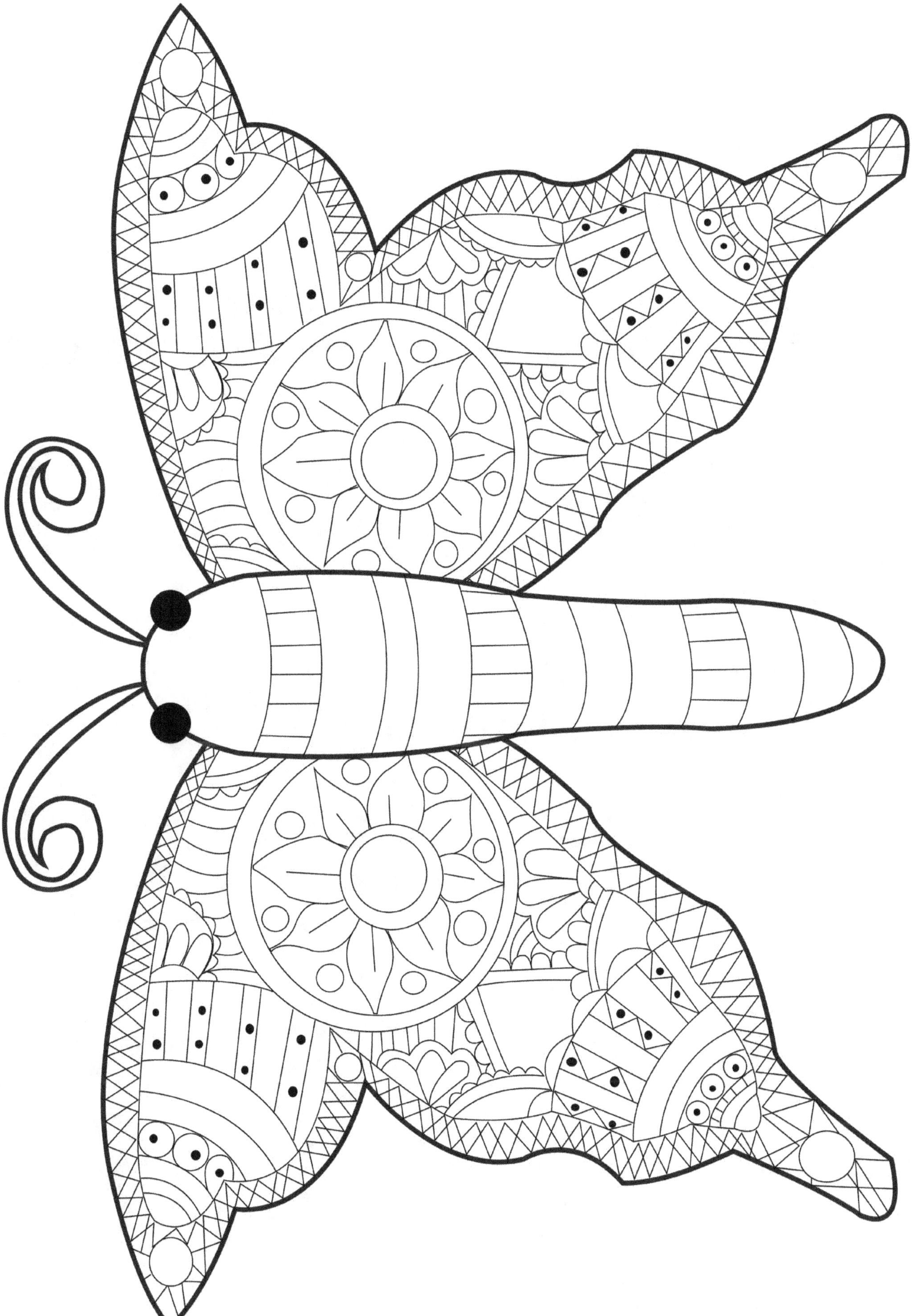

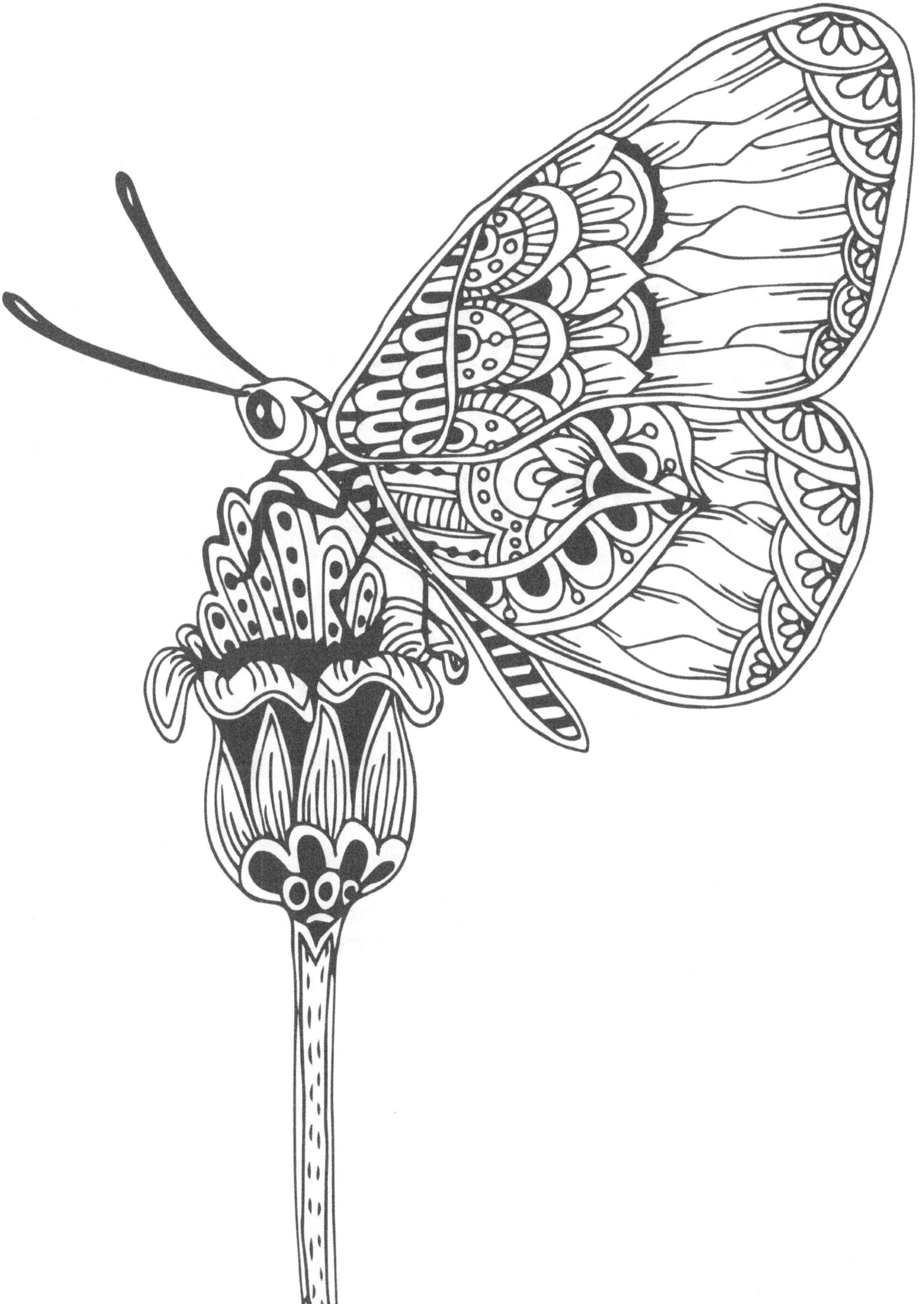

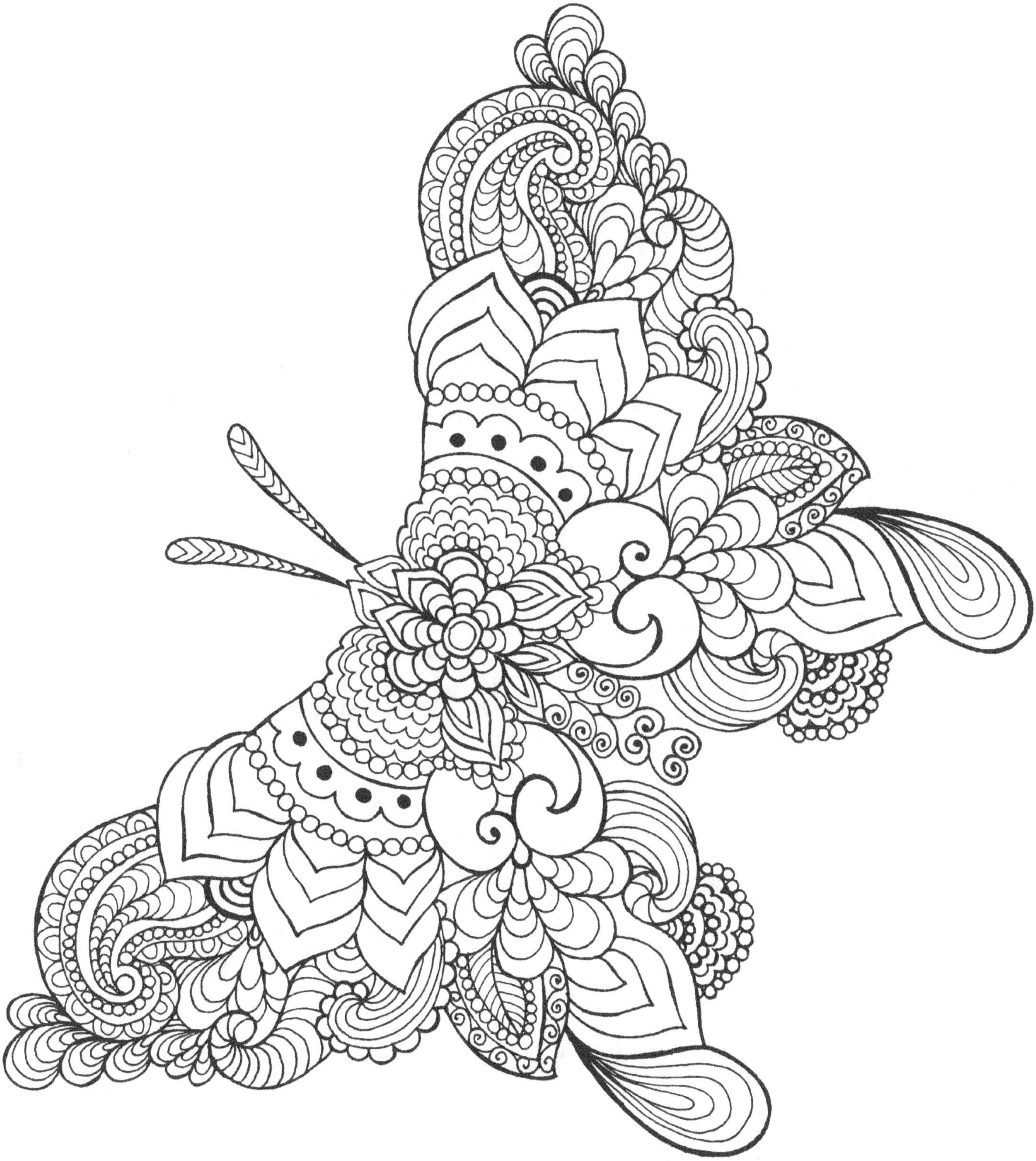

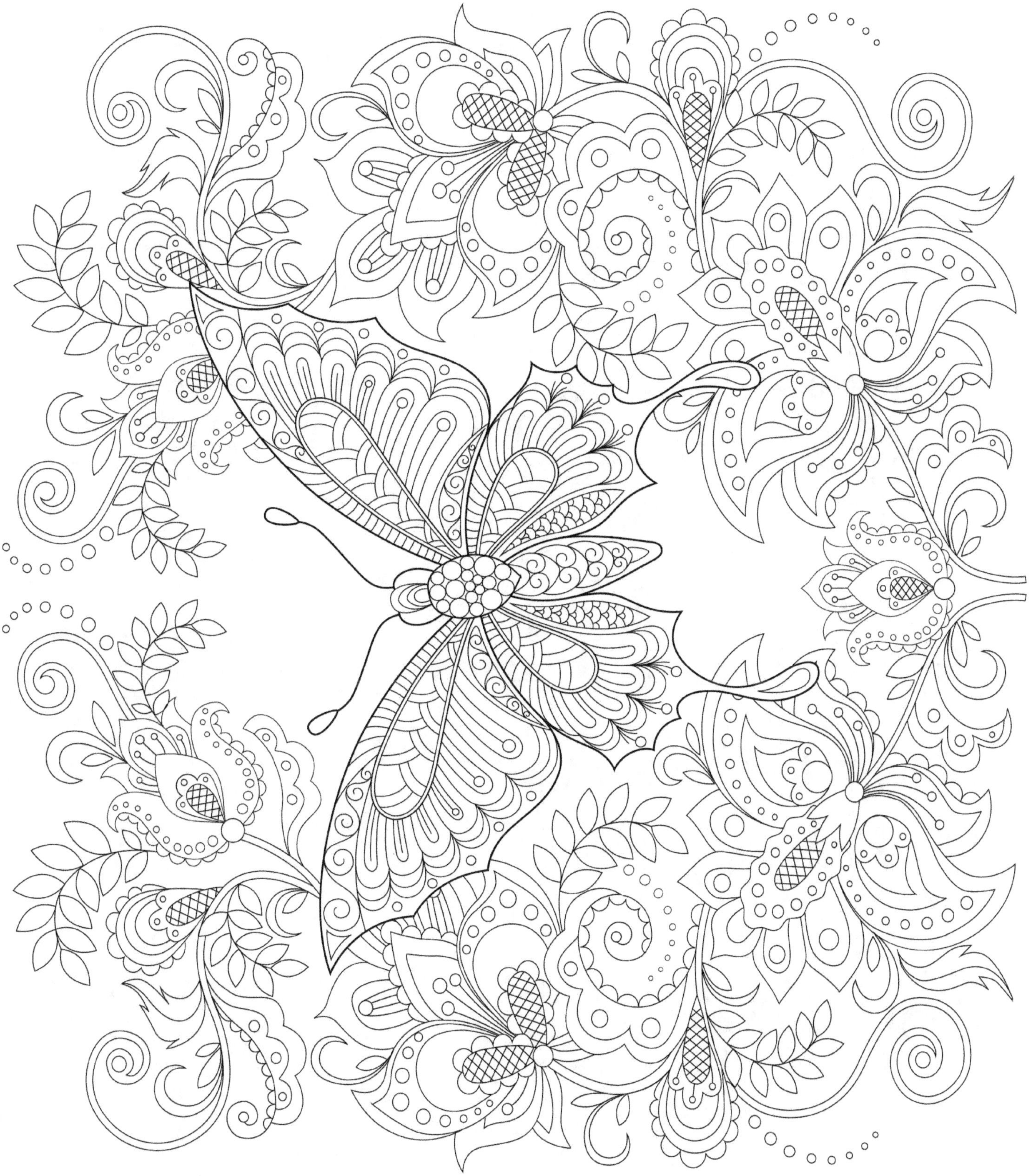

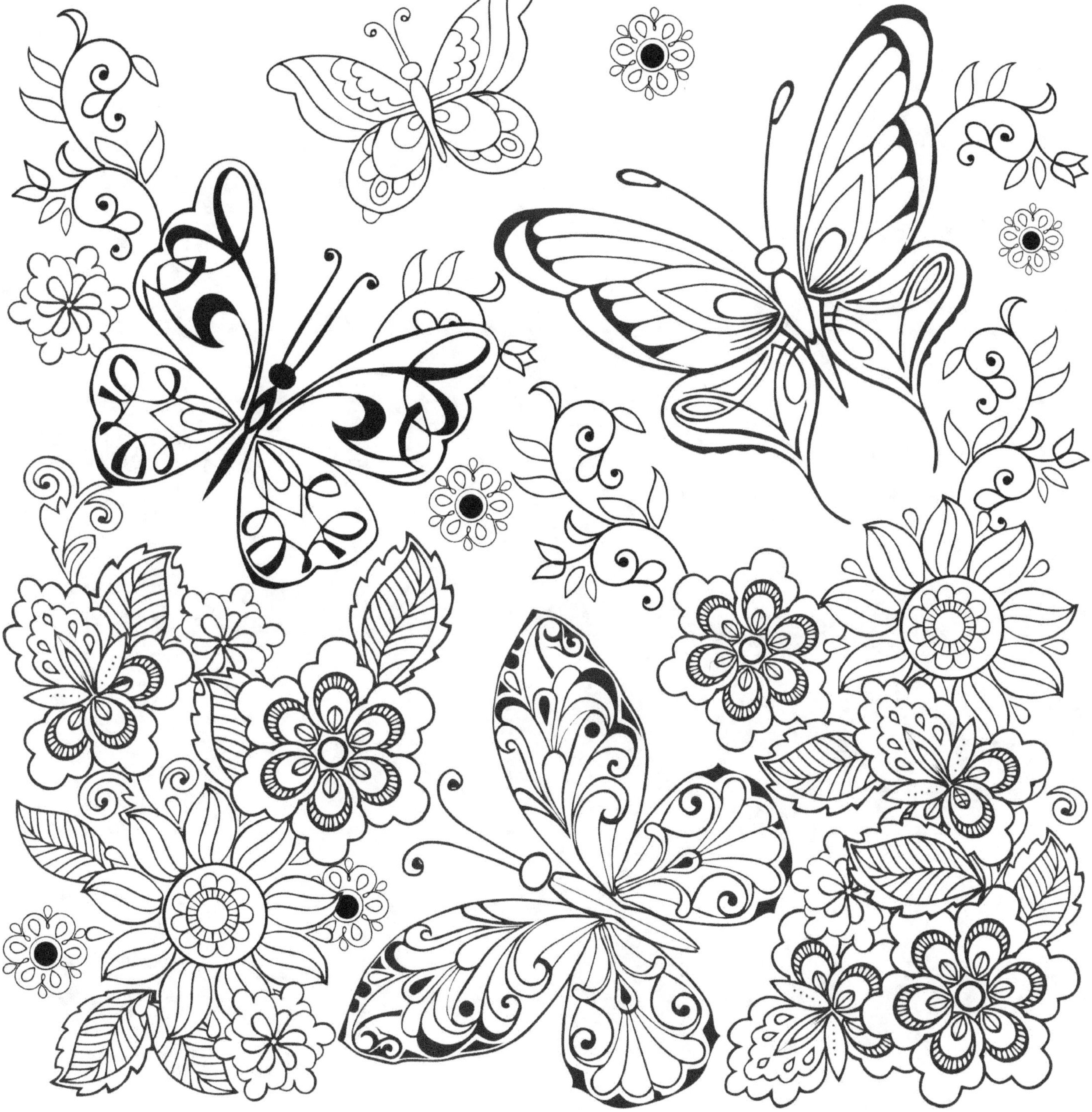

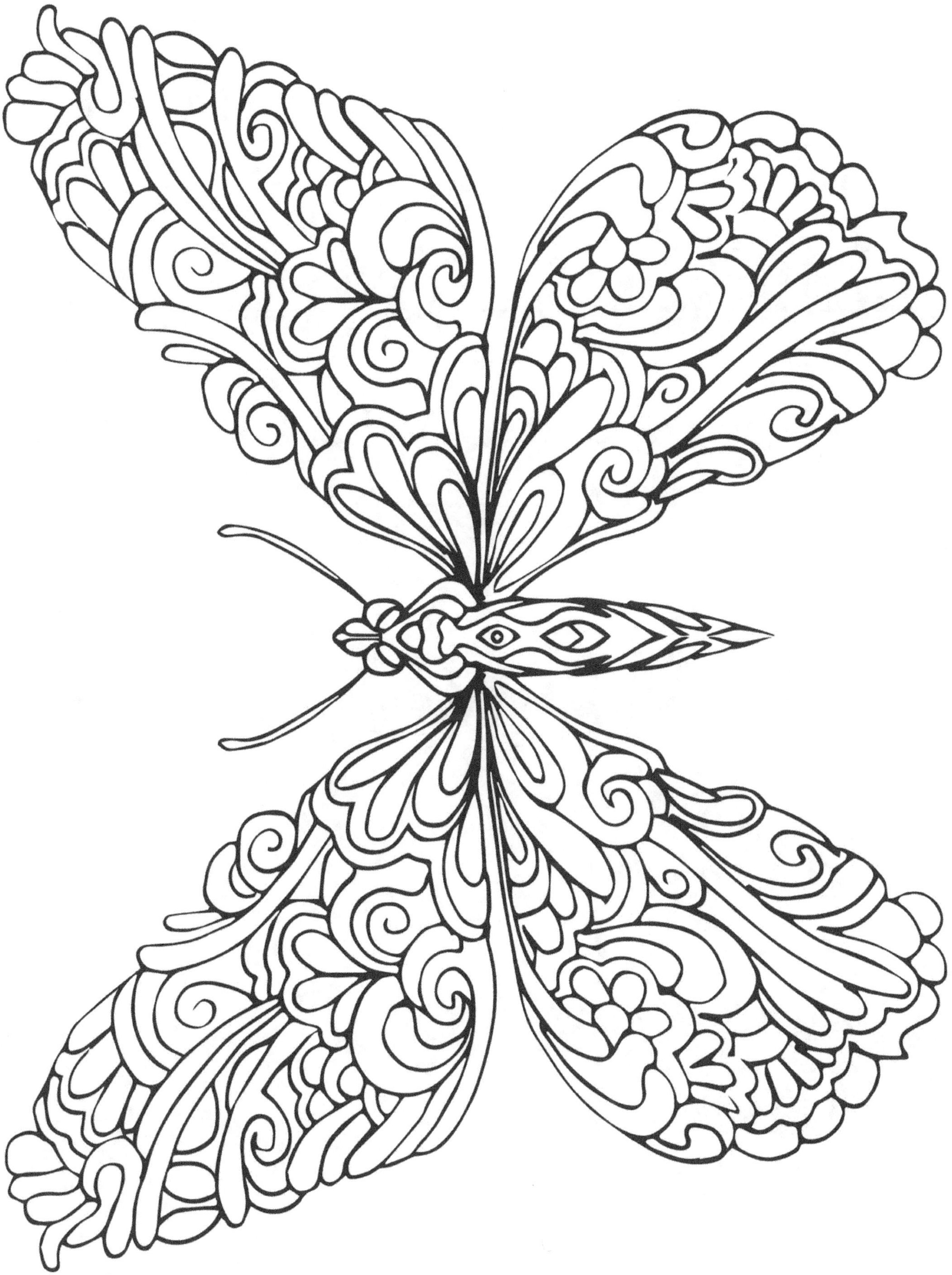

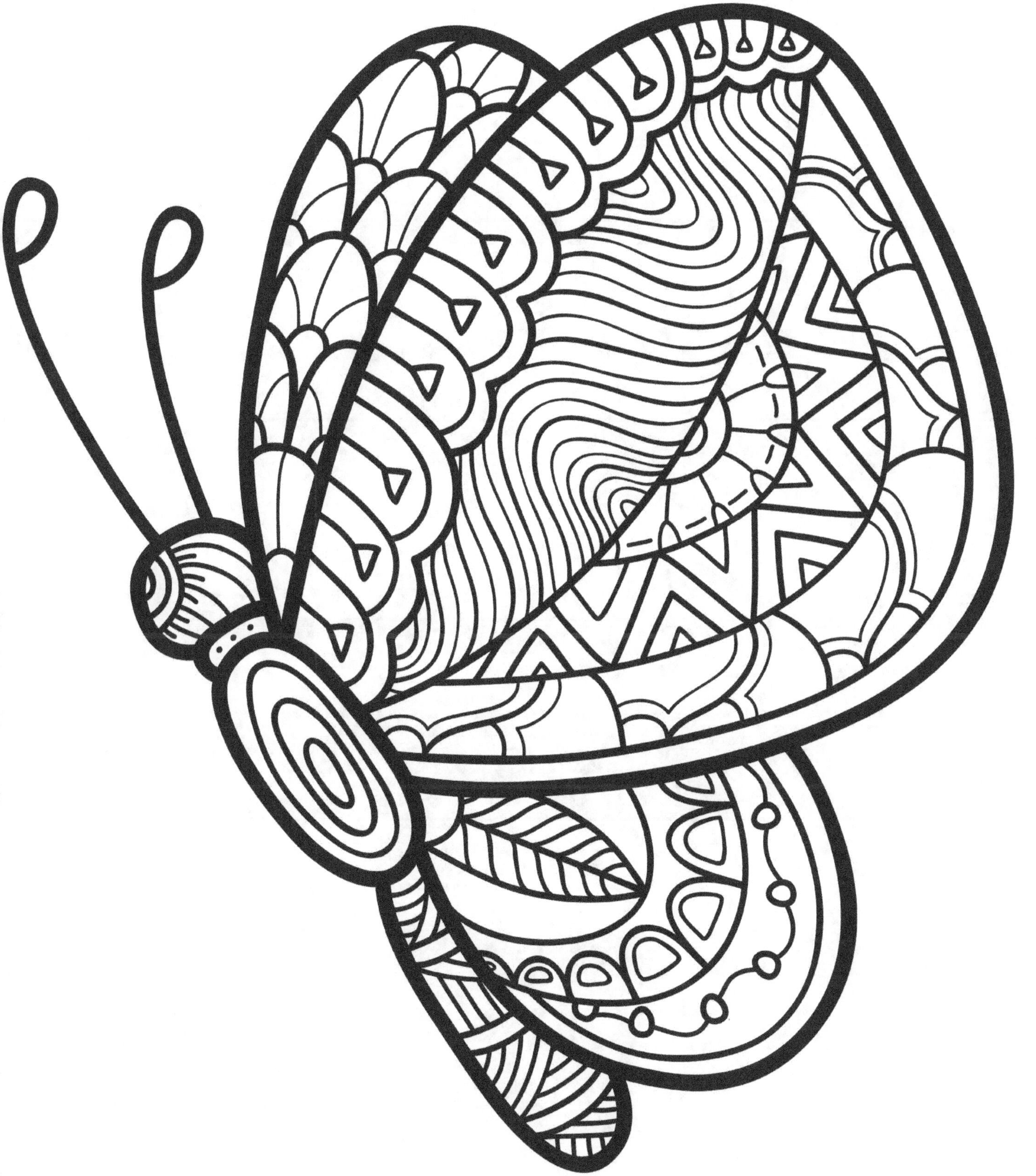

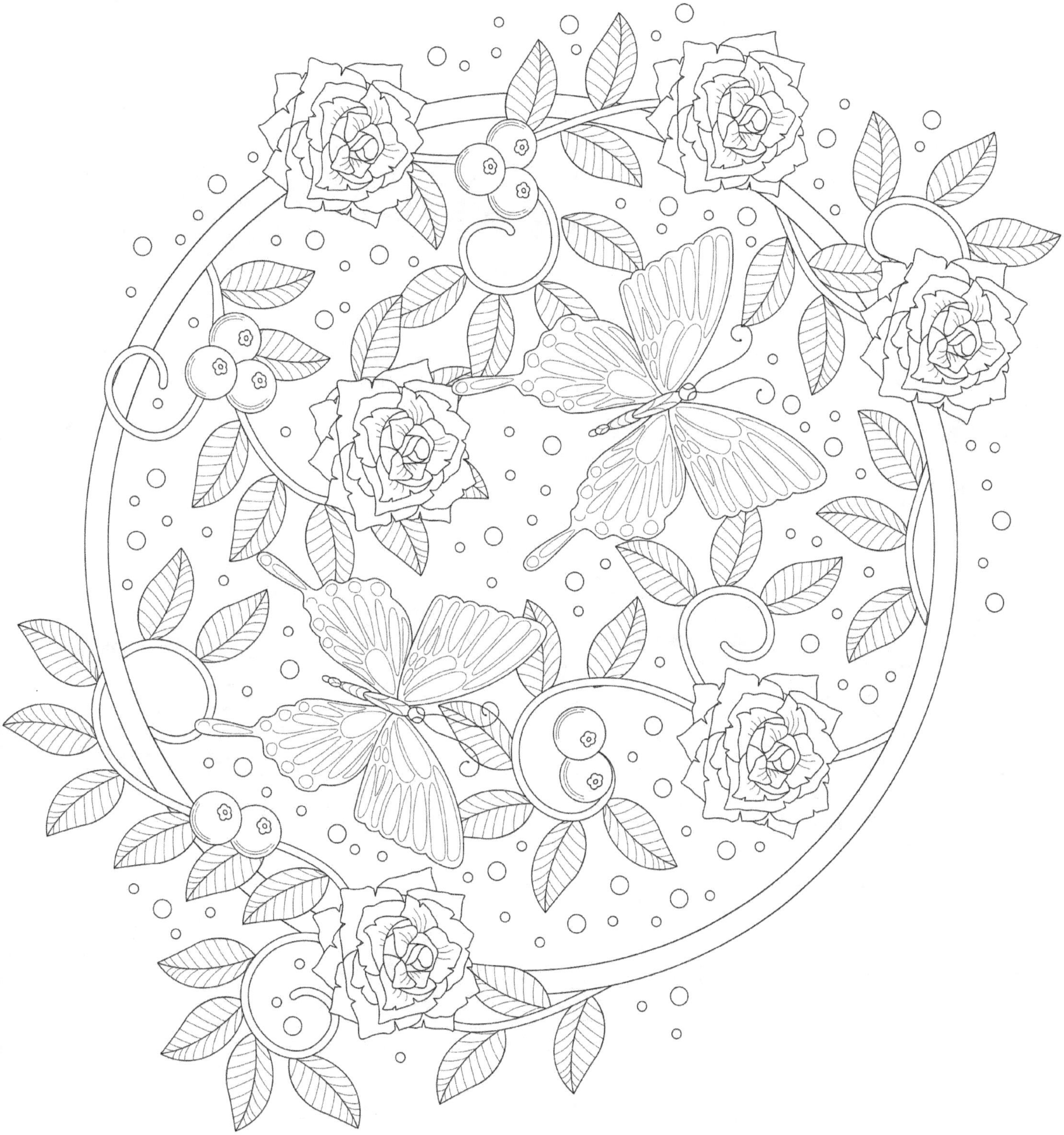

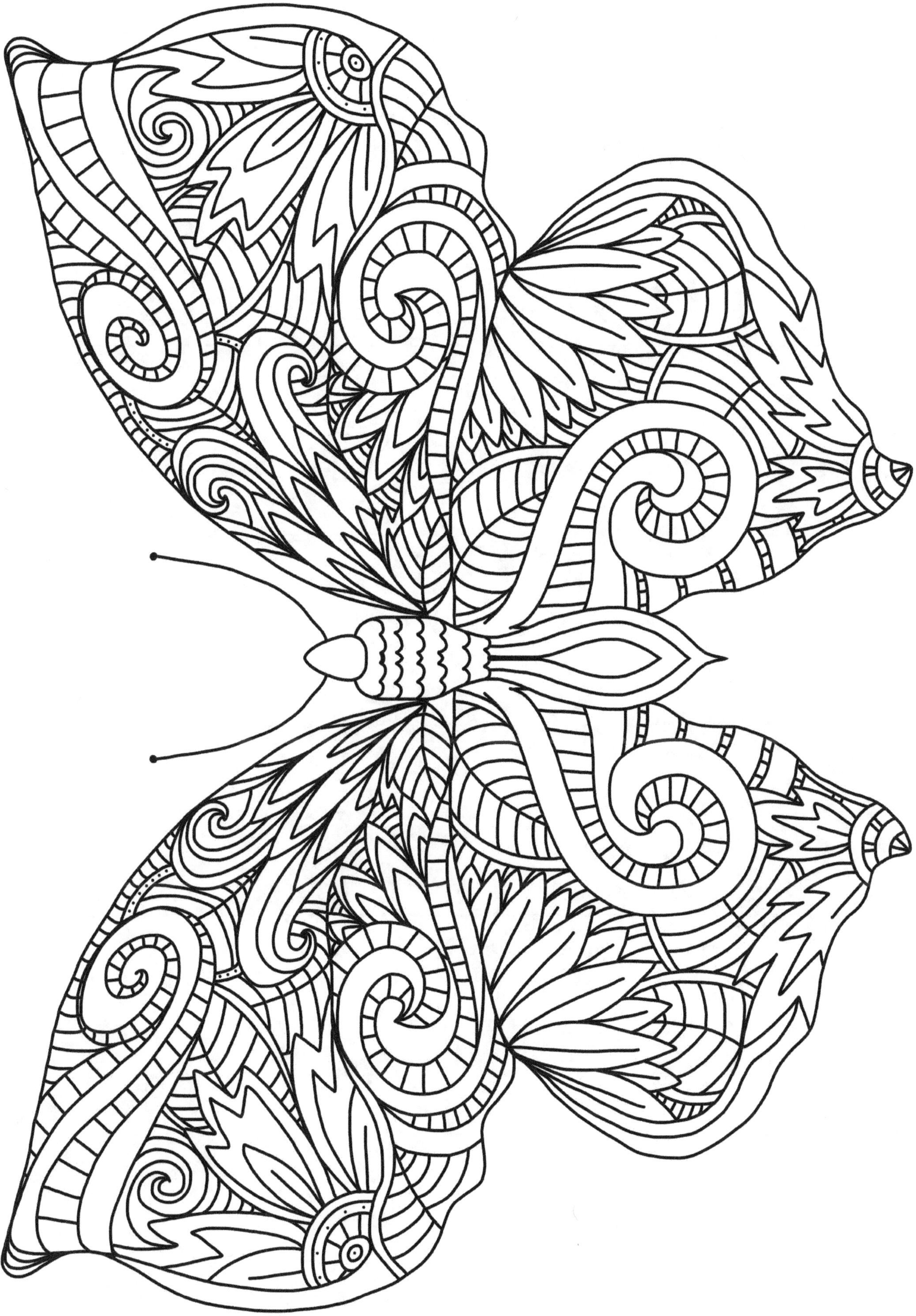

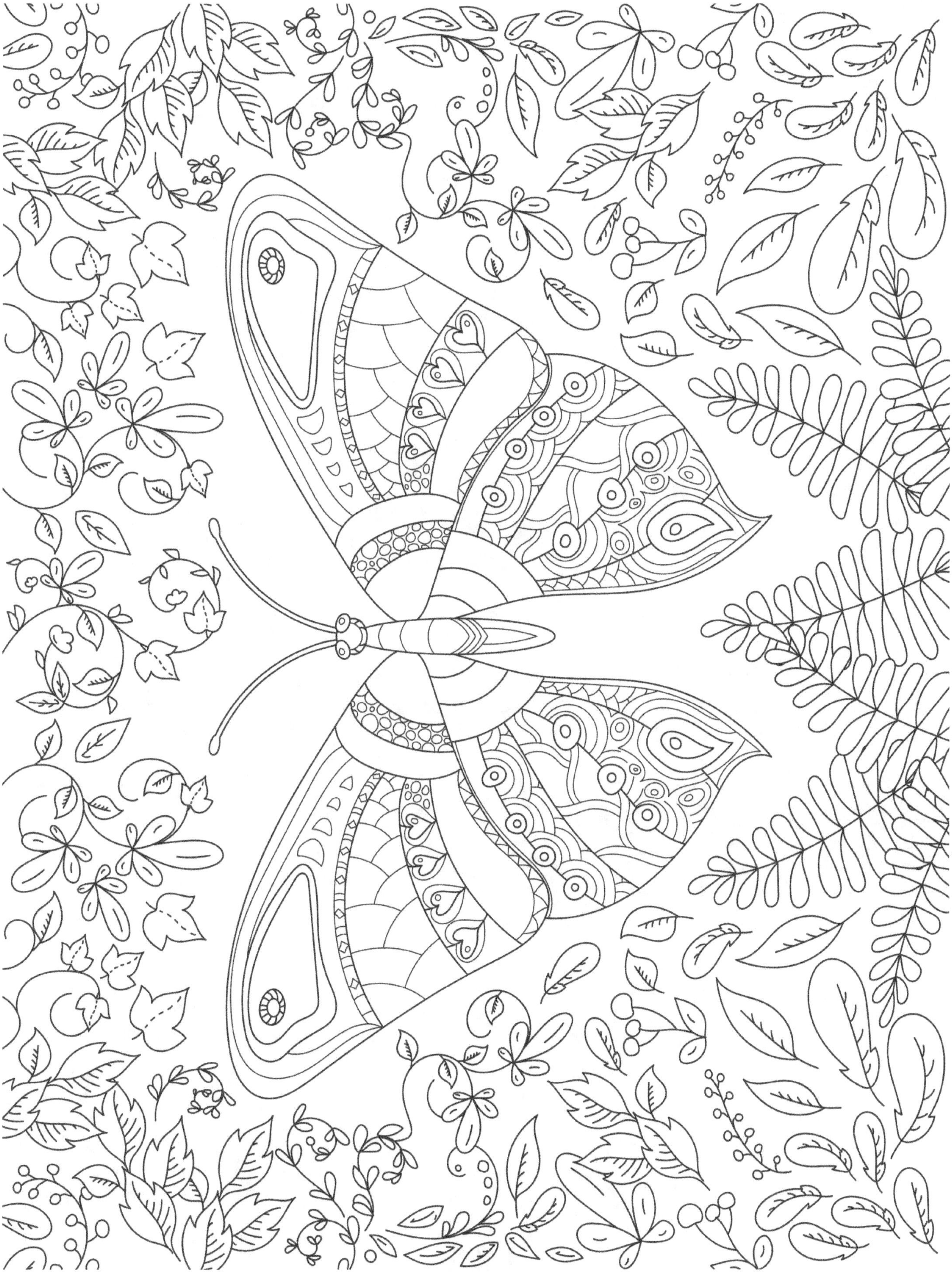

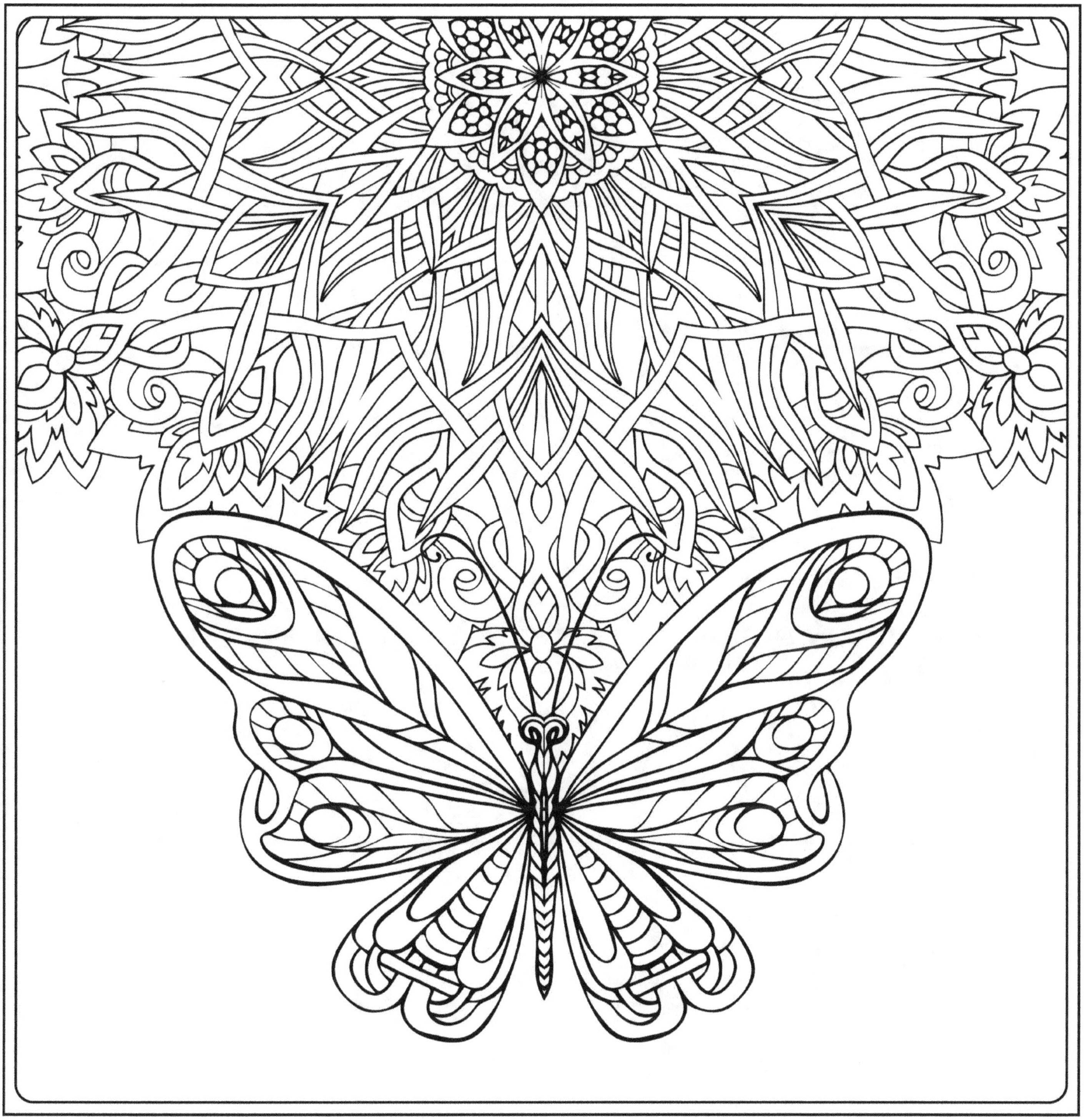

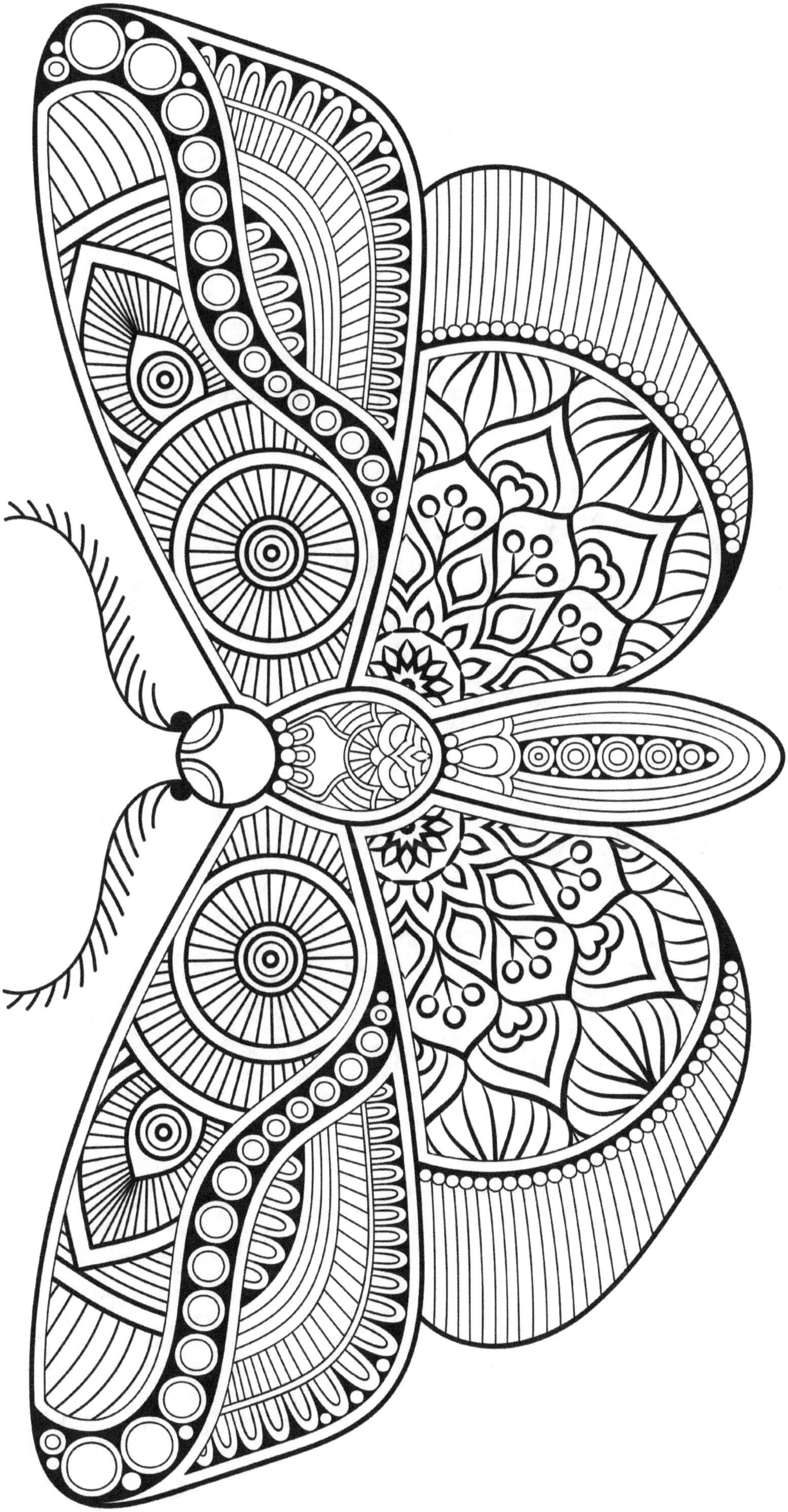

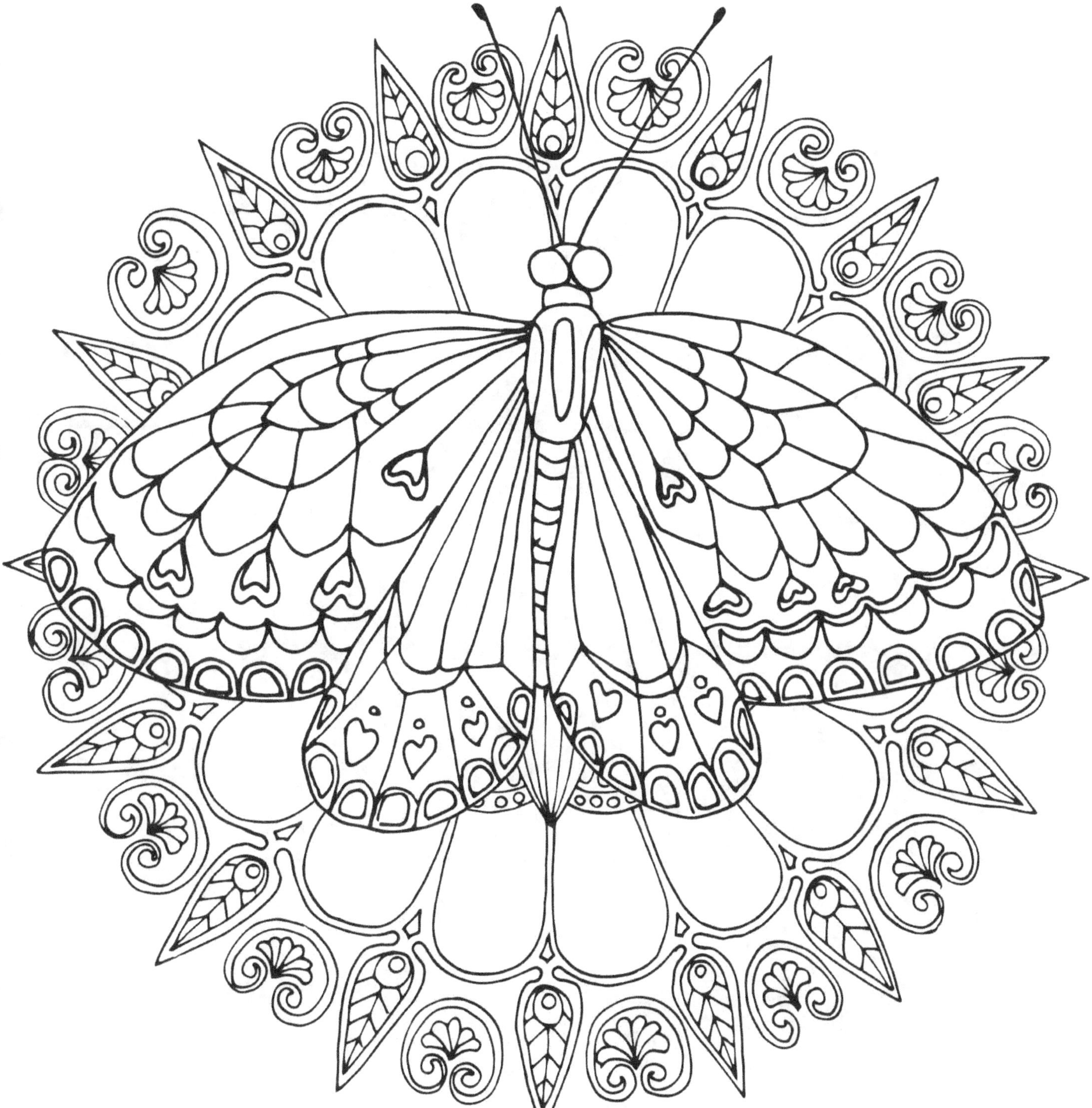

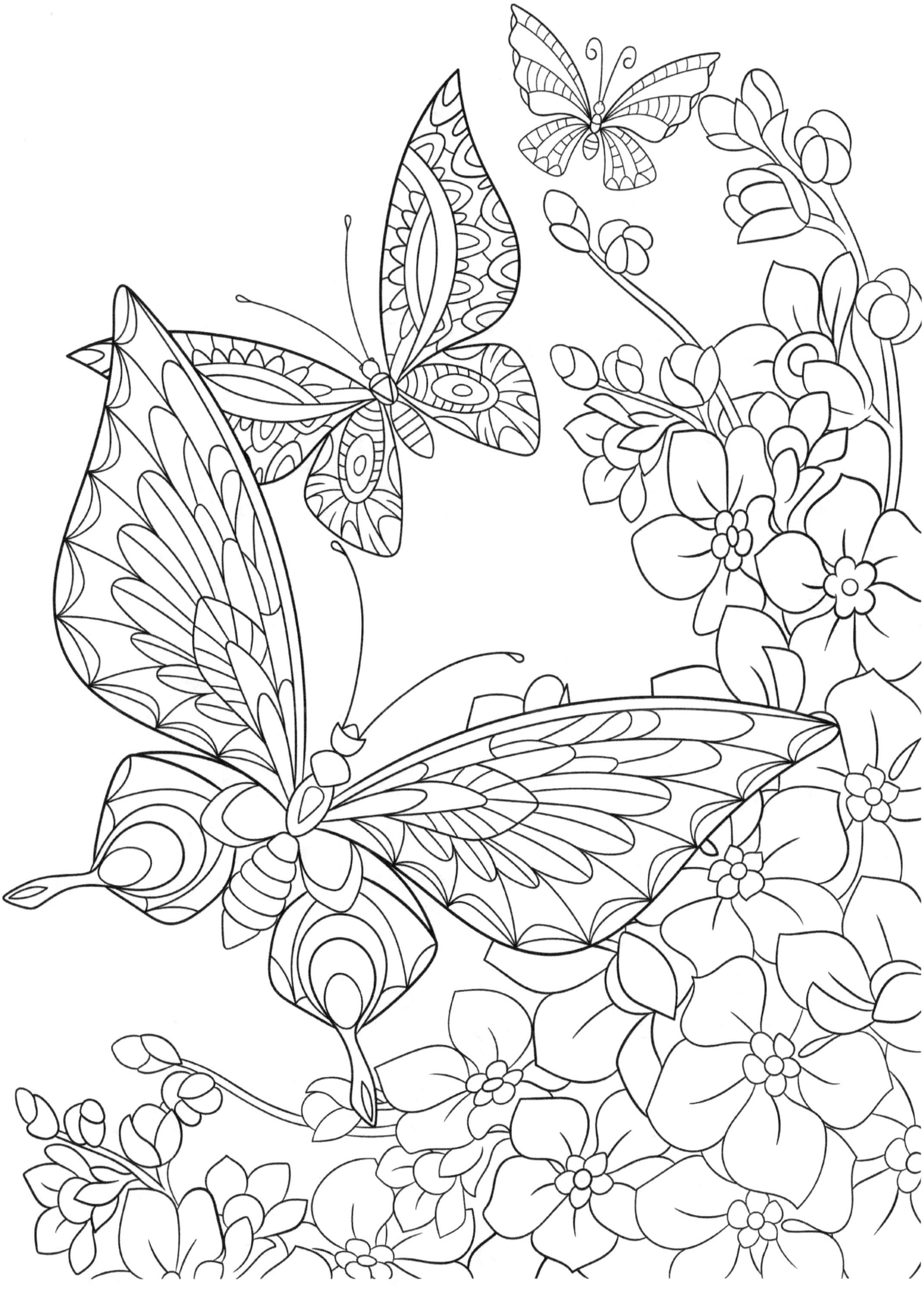

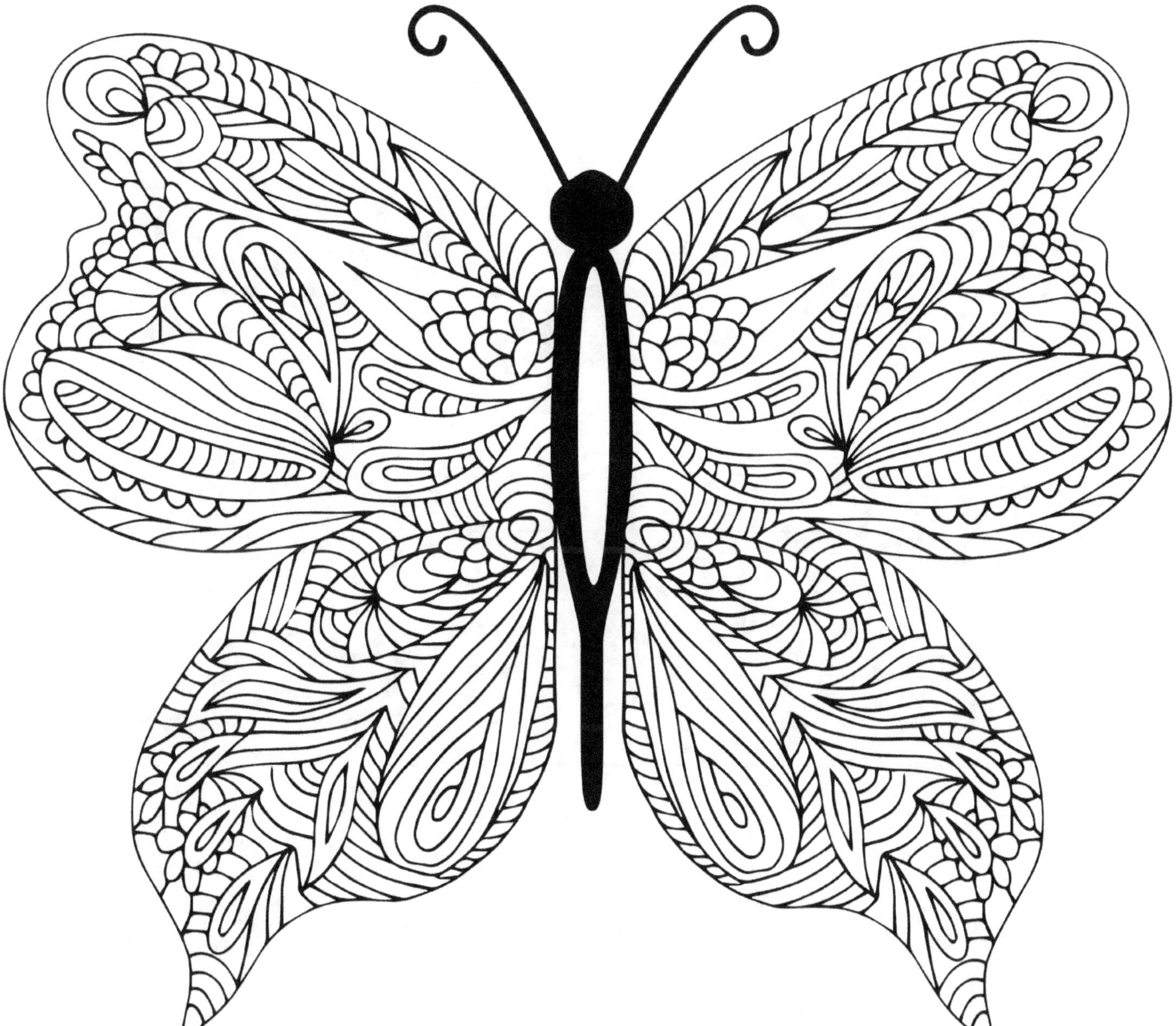

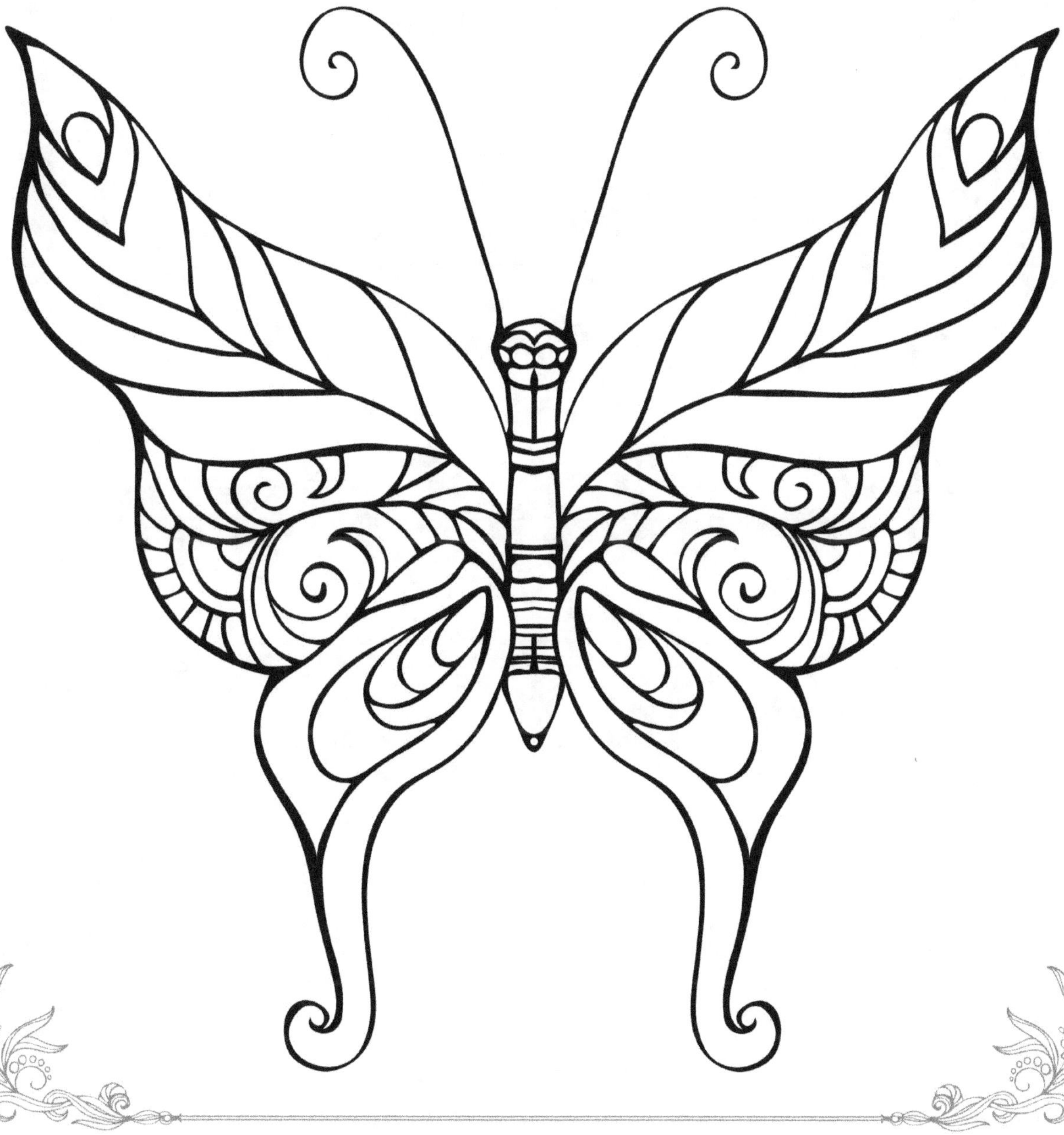

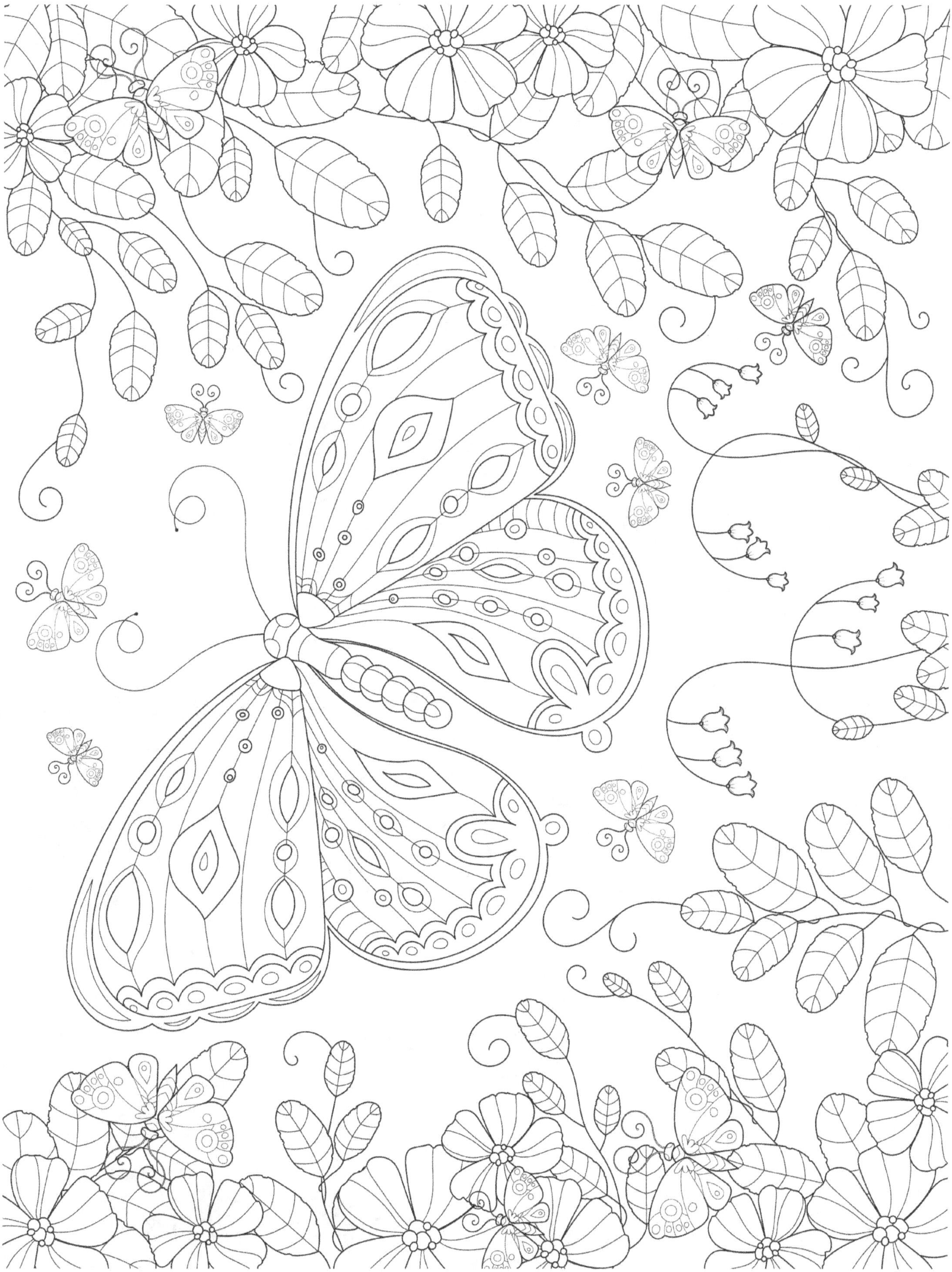

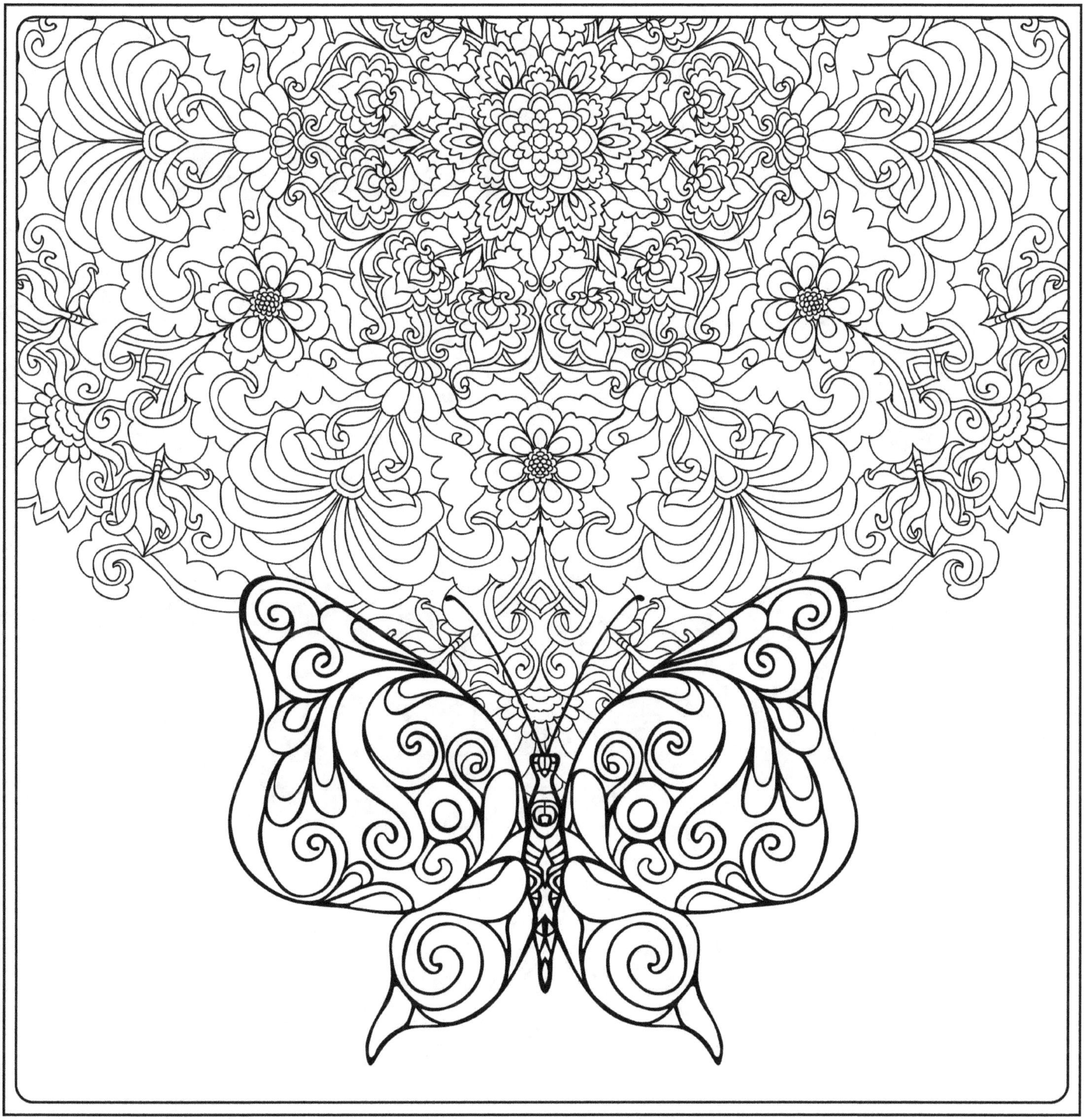

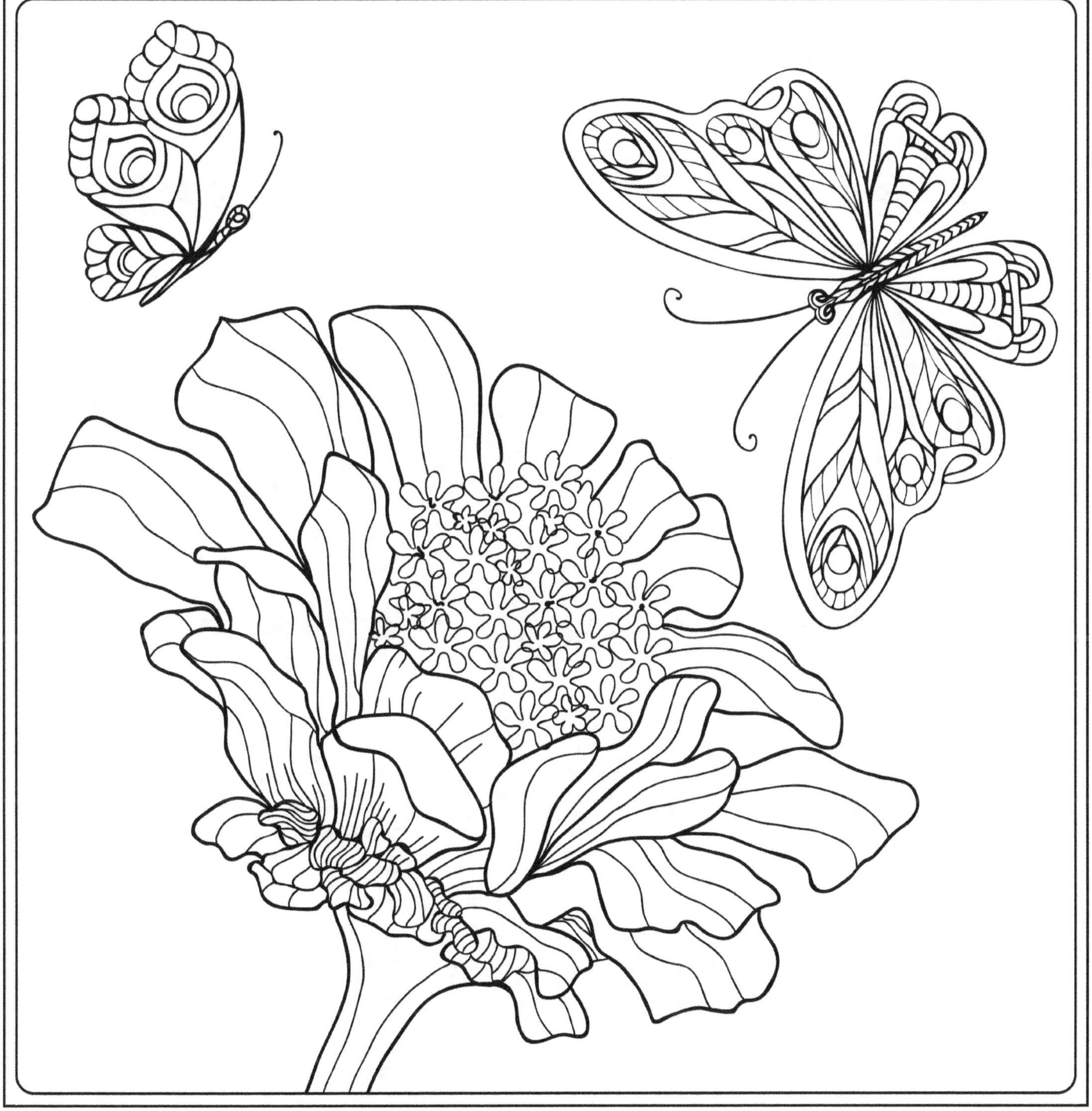

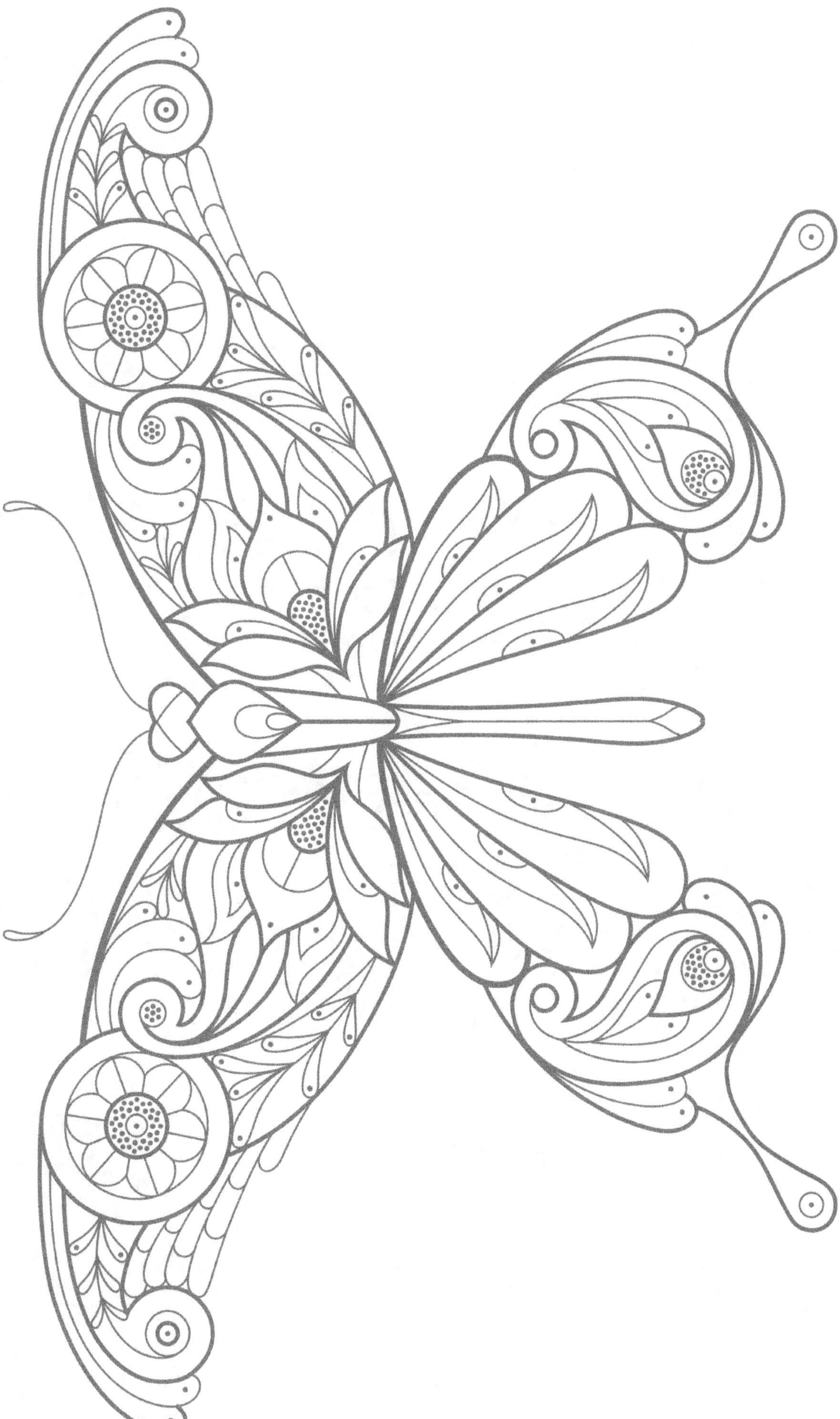

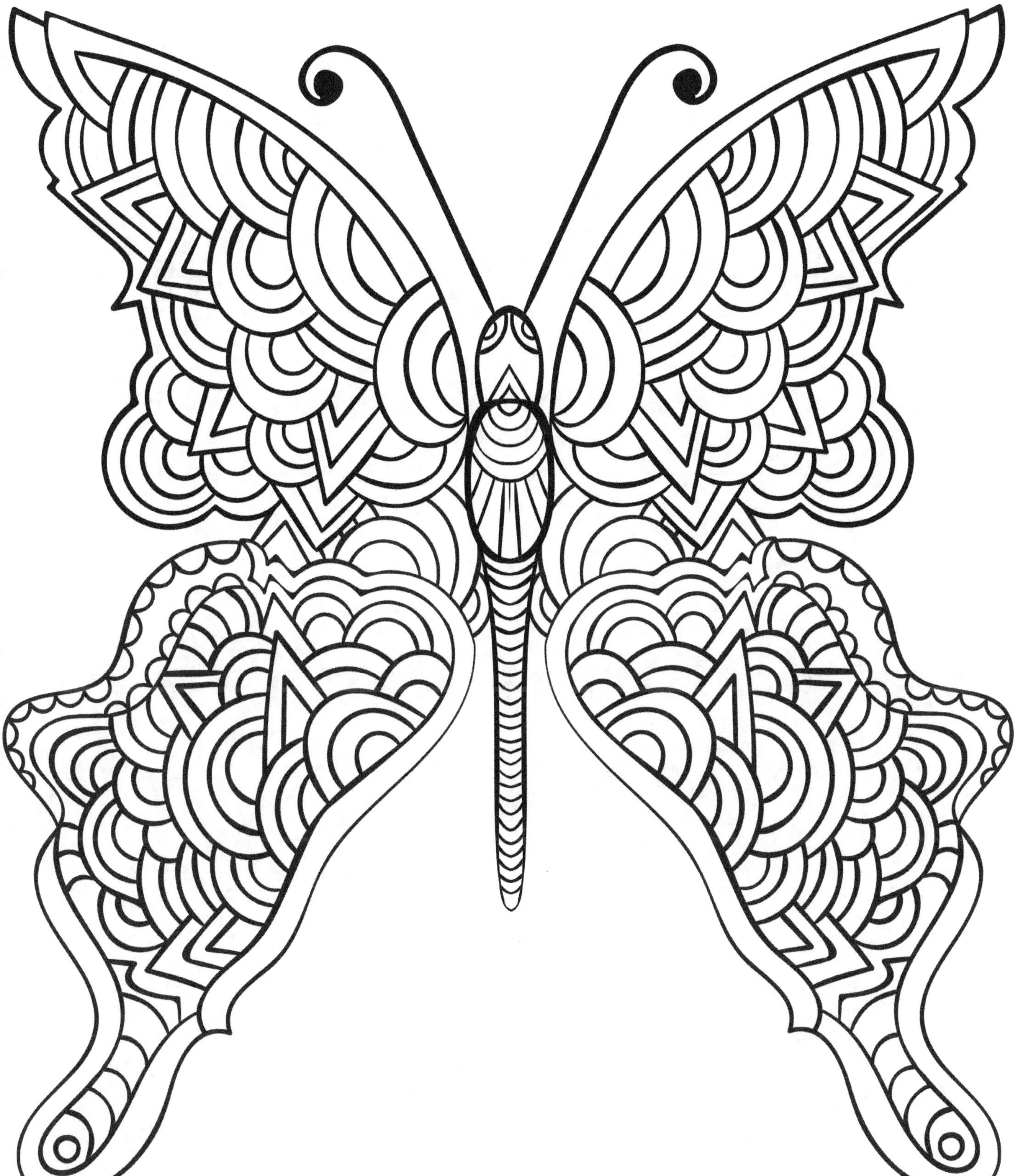

www.ingramcontent.com/pod-product-compliance
Lightning Source LLC
Chambersburg PA
CBHW080913170526
45158CB00008B/2090